PARADE

PARADE

MOUNTING YARDS.PADDOCKS.PARADE RINGS

PAUL ROBERTS & ISABELLE TAYLOR

Turnberry Consulting Ltd
41-43 Maddox Street, London, W1S 2PD, UK

Designed by Draught Associates
Printed by Blackmore

ISBN: 978-0-9569078-1-3

Contents

Introduction

Thoroughbred racing is, in many ways, an atypical sport. Not least, this is because the duration of sporting action is very short relative to the time span that the spectators spend at the venue. During an average seven-race-card meeting, the time elapsed in which horses are actually running may total only 10 to 15 minutes. The race, therefore, is only one aspect of the entertainment of the race day. For a racegoer, the day is composed of a series of experiences, each contributing to the unique theatre of the racing spectacle: eating, drinking and socialising; studying the racecard and staking a bet; listening to the sound of thundering hooves speeding past the grandstands; waiting at the parade ring rails to inspect the favourites at close quarters. For many, this latter experience is amongst the most compelling of the day's events.

Racing is one of the very few sports in which fans and bettors can appraise the competitors' well-being at close quarters just minutes before the contest begins. At the pre-parade and parade rings, they can watch as horses are saddled and prepared or as jockeys are whispered final instructions from trainers before mounting, enabling an analysis which can provide valuable clues as to the likely outcome of the race. No wonder then that these spaces make for some of the most revered destinations within the thoroughbred world.

Alongside the start and the finish of the races themselves, the display of the horses in the pre-parade and parade rings has long been a mainstay of the race-day ritual across the globe. It is essentially a two-stage rite: pre-saddling and post-saddling. As with other aspects of the sport, though, the process does differ from country to country. For example, both steps may take place in a single arena, as happens in North America, or there might be two separate rings, as characterises UK racing. In France, the first stage traditionally takes place away from the public gaze and horses enter the main parade ring ready saddled. Even the nomenclature varies between nations. To the British and Irish, the physical space in which horses are walked prior to being tacked is called the 'pre-parade ring', whereas racegoers in Australia would know this as the 'parade ring' or the 'birdcage'. In turn, while Australians recognise the ring in which saddled horses are walked and jockeys mount as the 'mounting yard', racegoers in the UK and Ireland designate this as the 'parade ring'. North Americans, meanwhile, term the parading arena as the 'paddock' or 'walking ring'.

Whatever the appellation though, parade rings are functionally integral to the mechanics of horse racing and an unmissable destination for the true racing fan. This study takes a sweeping survey of these fundamental, albeit somewhat overlooked, components of the physical environment of a racecourse. Part I introduces the origins of the parading ritual, its variations in different parts of the globe and the importance of the design of the rings themselves, before Part II profiles the parade rings of some of the sport's most renowned tracks, in a selection chosen to span the geographical and stylistic spectrum of this unique spatial type.

FASHIONS, FORMS AND FUNCTIONS

PASSES & JOCKEYS.

Parading begins

The first parade ring of the type known today appeared at the beginning of the twentieth century at the now defunct Gatwick Racecourse in the UK.[1] It was a permanent, fenced oval, designated as the site for the mounting and inspection of horses. A simple white rail divided the onlookers from the horses and their connections within the enclosure. The innovation was welcomed by contemporaries: 'Apart from the question of safety from horse's hooves,' enthused monthly sporting journal *Baily's Magazine of Sports & Pastimes* in 1907, 'the ring arrangement is the only one which permits of a clear view of the horses to be taken in comfort.'[2] Gatwick's precedent was soon followed by Newbury and Hurst Park.

However, the origin of the parade ring lies further back, in the nineteenth century. It was in this period that the idea first emerged of a designated space where horses could be saddled and observed by racegoers.

In the first half of the 1800s, thoroughbred racing was far from being well organised. Horses travelled between meetings on foot; perfidious dealings were rife. On race days, races were started by an official merely shouting 'go' at the top of his voice, starts were unpunctual, jockeys were rarely weighed, and horses were saddled anywhere and everywhere. However, slowly but surely, the sport grew less haphazard as a series of reforms began to be instituted to give form, order and rigour to the race day.

One of the most important of these measures was the evolution of the saddling paddock. As early as the 1820s, Epsom Racecourse could boast an early prototype located on the far side of the course in the grounds of a seventeenth-century hunting lodge, The Warren. 'It is a small, but picturesque bit of ground in the forest style, enclosed by a wall,' described *The North Wales Chronicle* in 1833.[3] Used on Oaks and Derby days, it cost a shilling to enter. 'There is nothing connected with the Derby Day which contains more interest, and which appears to be so little known, as this exhibition,' praised *The Bury and Norwich Post*. 'The horses are led several times round a small field, giving one the opportunity of judging of their respective symmetry and proportions... From this the horses, equipped for action, proceeded to the starting post.'[4] The arrangement was but an informal one, contingent upon the consent of The Warren's owner.

In the 1830s, routines and regulations began slowly and fitfully to be introduced to the pre-race procedure. At the North Wiltshire and Devizes Races in 1837, for example, it was stipulated that horses were 'to be saddled in front of the Grand Stand';[5] the succeeding year, Ascot issued an edict 'that horses in every race shall

Opposite: Saddling and mounting in front of the Royal Stand for the 1839 Gold Cup at Ascot. Previously, saddling had taken place anywhere within the racecourse

Above: Horses leaving the paddock at Newmarket's Rowley Mile course in 1895. The paddock had been in use since the early 1860s

be saddled in front of [the new weighing stand]'; and Worcester Racecourse followed by publicising that its August races were 'to start each day at one o'clock precisely, and the horses to be saddled in front of the Grand Stand'.[6] It seems that many horsemen turned a deaf ear to such directives. Nonetheless, these efforts mark early attempts to designate separate areas for saddling where horses could be observed by racegoers, and in so doing can be considered the starting point for the modern tradition of the parade ring.

From the 1840s, more racecourses across the UK gradually started to implement similar reforms, often under the impetus of the enterprising Jockey Club steward, Lord George Bentinck. Bentinck's resolve to rid the 'Sport of Kings' of dishonesty and disorder recast the pattern of racing. He instituted punctuality in starting for each race by fining clerks for each minute of delay; introduced the numbering of horses; pioneered the use of a starting flag; invented a horse box to transport his horses to races; and enforced both the public saddling of horses at a given place and their parade in front of the grandstand prior to racing. Saddling had hitherto occurred anywhere in the racecourse grounds, making it often a difficult task for jockeys to find their mounts on big race days, but under Bentinck's influence designated saddling paddocks were introduced at Goodwood, Aintree and Warwick.[7] In 1841, the *York Herald* described the newly created saddling enclosure at the Manchester Racecourse: 'In this enclosure, previous to each race, the horses will be

brought and saddled, similar to the usage at Goodwood and Liverpool [Aintree]; and, being, of open palisading, an excellent view will be obtained of the horses from the other stands, while the crowd will be effectively excluded.' This localisation and systematisation of the saddling procedure, together with the instigation of a formal procession in walk and canter in front of the stands, marked the beginning of the public pre-race rituals we know today.

The growing recognition amongst horsemen of the expedience of designating an enclosure where their equine athletes could be prepared led to the creation of more and more dedicated saddling paddocks across the UK: Newmarket (circa 1858), York (1875) and Bath (1879) were examples. *The Sheffield and Rotherham Independent* reported in 1871 that a saddling paddock, measuring 140 metres by 34 metres (460 feet by 112 feet), was one of the most notable improvements to have been made that year at Doncaster Racecourse, 'the want of which has always been much felt'. It included a timber shed, 62 metres (204 feet) long, containing saddling stalls and a small refreshment booth. Saddling sheds were common features, while standalone weighing rooms and jockeys' rooms were also often present.

The new feature was also quickly adopted beyond the UK shores, particularly in Australia where racing had been wholeheartedly and rapidly embraced. When the Australian Jockey Club hosted its first race meeting at Randwick in Sydney in 1860, the racecourse included a

saddling paddock behind its grandstand. The same year Flemington Racecourse was remodelled and a paddock was laid out to the west of its new stands. In 1861, the erstwhile rustic New Town Racecourse in Tasmania erected a weighing house, jockeys' room and saddling paddock in time for its Australian Championship Meeting.

The imposition of rules governing the pre-race preparations initially drew grumblings from the racing community, especially in Britain, and they were often breached. However, by 1899 the saddling rite was a regulated aspect of the British race-day protocol. That year, it was mentioned for the first time in the Jockey Club's rules of racing:

> The Clerk of the Course shall see that at all meetings where a charge is made for the admission of the public to the Paddock, all horses running at the Meeting shall be brought into the Paddock, and the attendants be provided with badges bearing numbers corresponding with those on the card.

Why the rule was applied to only those meetings where the public paid to enter the paddock is not explained, but it is, in essence, this directive that still prevails. The wording has, over time, been amended and expanded. A consequential addition was made in 1948, for example, when it was stipulated that a specific parade ring had to be provided:

> The Clerk of the Course shall see that a parade ring is provided in the paddock. All horses running at the meeting shall be saddled in the appointed place and brought into the parade ring a reasonable time before the signal to mount is given.

Opposite: Flemington's paddock – known as the birdcage – depicted in 1890

Form and function

Opposite: The tree-lined pre-parade ring at Newmarket's Rowley Mile course creates a tranquil environment for the horses' pre-race preparations

Today, British racecourses are governed by clear rules which stipulate what occurs before horses proceed to the start. Here, custom dictates that handlers lead runners around a pre-parade ring before taking them to be saddled in stalls in or adjacent to the ring. By a specified time, horses must arrive in the main parade ring. The ringing of a bell signals the moment for jockeys to mount, and thenceforth proceed to the track.

Yet, while this routine is performed nationwide, the design of the spaces in which it is performed varies widely in size, shape, position and aesthetic pretensions. At Doncaster, the parade ring is located in front of the stands; at York, it is sited at the end of the stands alongside the track; Ascot's parade ring sits immediately behind its grandstand. Sandown has a triangular ring; at Windsor, it is circular; while Goodwood's is a more conventional oval shape. At Aintree, Newmarket's Rowley Mile, and Kempton Park, the winners' enclosure is housed within the main ring; conversely, at Thirsk, Epsom and Ripon, the winners' enclosure is independent. And while the pre-parade and parade rings of UK racecourses exhibit enormous variation, when considered on an international scale, the differences in design become even greater.

From its genesis in the UK, the parading ritual spread across the globe to become an integral part of the sport worldwide. In Australia and New Zealand, turfites have followed their British counterparts in adopting a pattern of distinct parade and pre-parade rings.[8] In North America, a single enclosure – termed the paddock – serves to combine both functions, comprising walking ring and saddling stalls, and sited behind the stands.

There are no hard and fast rules governing the siting, size or shape of a parade ring, but a successful design must fulfil certain basic requirements. A parade ring needs to:

- be accessibly positioned so it is close to the weighing-in building and easily approachable for racegoers;
- be a safe environment for horses, horsemen and the public;
- have defined (ideally segregated) access to the track and stables, and an access route for emergency vehicles such as ambulances;
- afford good sightlines for racegoers;
- be sufficiently sized for the maximum number of runners that the racecourse hosts in any one race;
- strike a balance between being atmospheric for the racegoer and calming for the horse.

The location of the parade ring within a racecourse estate can have a tangible impact upon the experiences of both racegoers and horses and horsemen. The journey which horses must traverse from stable to track via pre-parade and parade ring, for instance, can have a substantial bearing upon the thoroughbreds' performances. The issue is not one of the distance of the route; a 20-metre long passage would be too far for the excitable runners if it passed a brass band, for example. The critical

factor is that the horses' progress from stable to track is designed to be as calming and safe as possible, and this includes the parade ring.

The siting of the ring is often a function of land availability. Many of the world's oldest tracks, such as Ascot (founded 1711), had well-established built environments long before the advent of parade rings in the early twentieth century, and so the latter were typically inserted at the far ends of the grandstand complexes alongside the track. This arrangement often impeded the spectator experience of the parade ring, involving lengthy treks for many from the stands to ring to betting window and back to the stands again in time for the race. When wholly new racecourses unrestricted by extant site conditions were built in the twentieth century, such as the Hipódromo da Gavea in the 1920s, Santa Anita Park in the 1930s or Sha Tin in the 1970s, parading activities tended instead to be located to the rear of the grandstand in order to maximise viewing potential.

Recent years have seen a trend to reposition main parade rings at older tracks to more central, 'spectator friendly' spots directly behind the grandstand. Chantilly, for example, was granted permission to displace a public road that skirted the rear of its grandstand in order to create the space necessary to relocate its parade ring from its trackside position to a more accessible one behind the stand, opened in 2007. The year before, Ascot completed a wholesale redevelopment which saw its parade ring moved from the west end of the Royal Enclosure stands to a new site immediately behind the grandstand. Veterans lamented the loss of the much-cherished ring with its canopy of mature trees, but its current setting evinced a more egalitarian attitude to facilitating access for all racegoers. Its position, moreover, meant that the balconies along the rear elevation of the grandstand provided additional viewing space, supplementing the stepped terraces that encircled the ring.

Ensuring clear sightlines and ample viewing capacity are decisive requirements of the spectator's parade ring experience. They make for vital factors in the design of new rings. Many larger courses surround their main parade rings with stepped viewing platforms to facilitate visibility. Ascot's steeply raked terraces accommodate up to 8,000 spectators and, furthermore, serve to amplify the sense of drama of big race days. Royal Randwick's 2013 remodelling realised a new main ring (with a 4,500 capacity) so designed with this in mind that the arena was christened the 'Theatre of the Horse'.

Safety too must be considered in the design of parade rings, both in terms of the horse and horsemen and the public. Sturdy barriers ensure the two parties are separated by an adequate distance; the horse paths themselves are customarily paved with non-slip, shock-absorbing surfaces; while the rings must also be large enough to safely host the maximum field sizes and their connections.

The sizes of parade rings vary widely from course to course, country to country. In the UK, Newmarket and Aintree can host up to 40-horse fields, and therefore need parade rings that are spacious enough to cater for this number in safety. In the US, conversely, barring the exception of the Kentucky Derby, field sizes typically reach only 12 or so at a maximum, meaning that large rings are not required.

Opposite: The pre-parade procession at Catterick Racecourse

Above: The 18-sided indoor
paddock at Laurel Park, built in the
1920s, is still in use today

Opposite: The indoor paddock
at Hollywood Park (opened
1938) was integrated within
the structure of the grandstand
itself. It was in use until a fire in
1949 destroyed the grandstand,
after which it was replaced by
a more conventional outdoor
walking ring

Of course, there are also wide divergences in
aesthetic pretensions between parade rings
worldwide. Some rings and their environs
are adorned with flowers, trees and statues.
Sandown Park boasts its Rhododendron Walk,
and the pre-parade ring at Newmarket's July
Course is cherished for the dappled sunlight
created by its cathedral-like canopy of trees.
At the centre of Belmont Park's paddock
stands one of the turf's most celebrated
sculptures, a bronze effigy of Secretariat in
mid-stride, installed in 1974, whilst Ascot's
parade ring is home to a statue of Yeats (2011),
commemorating his unique achievement as
four-time winner of the Gold Cup.

Perhaps the accolade for the greatest aesthetic
innovation in parade ring design should go
to Hollywood Park. When the glamorous
Californian track was opened in 1938, it
included the novel feature of an indoor
paddock. Indoor paddocks as such were not a
wholly new phenomenon. At Laurel Park, for
instance, a polygonal timber paddock building
was opened in the 1920s, adjacent to the west
wall of the grandstand. Although sheltered
by a low, sweeping roof, its sides were largely
unenclosed. Unlike the freestanding Laurel Park
paddock though, Hollywood Park's ring was
fully enclosed, integrated into the centre of the
long, sleek grandstand. It was a circular, dome-
covered space well insulated for soundproofing
to ensure a settled environment for the horses.
It was beautified with box hedge, while railed,
raked steppings encircled the perimeter from
which racegoers could observe favourites at
close hand. When the grandstand was destroyed
by fire in 1949, the indoor ring was lost too, and
its replacement took the form of a traditional
grassed walking ring behind the grandstand.

The importance of the parade ring

Whatever the form they assume and whatever aesthetic aspirations they boast, parade rings have become an inveterate part of the race-day custom. They operate, in a sense, on two levels: the functional and the festal. For the trainers, owners, jockeys and horses, parade rings are associated with race practicalities. It is here that horses are prepared and that jockeys meet trainers and connections for final pre-race instructions. They afford an arena for trainers to oversee the preparation of the horse and, furthermore, ensure that this is a transparent process for the racegoers. They physically separate the horses and the public, thereby facilitating the safety of both parties, and, in providing a defined setting for the pre-race activities, they assist in control of race timings.

The pre-parade ring, too, also serves to smooth the way for punctual timing through its function as an intermediary zone. This is particularly valuable if the stables are at a distance from the parade ring. The essential veterinary and farrier facilities are typically located at the pre-parade ring, in addition to the open and closed boxes for saddling.

Furthermore, the festive dimension of the parade ring is also increasingly being embraced and amplified. They are a forum for heightening the atmosphere of the race-day experience, acting as a visual interest and serving to build the connection between the public and the horse and its entourage. This means they are regularly a focal point for media coverage and are often used as sites for television interviews.

Over the past century, the arena of the parade ring has become increasingly formalised, governed by the rules and regulations of the sport, while its form has grown more and more sophisticated. From grassed ovals enclosed by simple wooden railings, they have evolved to become amphitheatres appointed with reinforced railings and often specialised non-slip paving designed to ensure a safe, serene atmosphere for horses whilst maximising the viewing potential for the spectators.

This is symptomatic of the changing psyche of racecourse environments as a whole. Over the past century, they have become progressively more composite. The accumulating pace of technology and increasing competition for consumers' time and money have transformed the nature of racecourses. To compete with other forms of leisure, it has become insufficient to cater for the veteran racegoer alone; racecourses must now be destinations for entertainment that entice and engage all sectors of society, even those with minimal knowledge and

Above: In 2015, York Racecourse completed a remodelling of its paddock which enhanced its draw to racegoers through improved viewing and associated hospitality provision

interest in the sport. As the architect of Ascot's 2006 redevelopment, Rod Sheard, observed, 'selling an "experience" is the core business of any stadium'.[9]

Pre-parade and parade rings have a crucial part to play in this. Together with the grandstand and the track, they create the stage on which the spectacle of the race day is enacted. Places of colour, intimacy, anticipation and adrenaline, they are theatres of the thoroughbred. 'Parade rings provide a focal point for racegoers,' Brendan Phelan, architect of a recent redevelopment of York Racecourse, has commented. 'They have become a hospitality destination, as an alternative to the track, which has led to a growth in associated restaurants, champagne bars and pavilions.'[10] The parade ring scheme at Goodwood (completed 2001), for instance, incorporated three hospitality pavilions as an integral part of the design.

When considering a parade ring, the foremost concern must always be whether it provides a secure, tranquil environment appropriate for the saddling and mounting of horses that encourages the best jockeys, owners and trainers to return. However, a well-designed parade ring can also function as an indispensible cog in building the momentum of the race day, investing it with a drama that beguiles, enlivens and ensures racegoers are drawn back time and time again.

CASE STUDIES

Aintree Racecourse
Liverpool, UK

Saddling paddocks or enclosures began to be introduced at Britain's racecourses from around 1840, and Aintree, which opened its doors in 1829, was one of the first to embrace this new development. Moreover, the racecourse boasted one of the earliest parade rings. Although the first example is held to have been that established at the now-defunct Gatwick Racecourse in the early 1900s, Aintree followed quickly on its heels creating a spacious, rectangular ring in 1908 behind the grandstand.

In the late 1940s, the ring shrunk in size. Due to a road-widening scheme, part of it was lost, transforming it from a rectangle to a square. Partially surrounded by mature trees, it occupied a corner site bounded by the busy Ormskirk Road and the entrance road to the racecourse. By the turn of the twenty-first century, this location and loss of space was proving challenging when it came to hosting Aintree's greatest event, the Grand National.

Many racecourses describe certain events in their calendar as unique, but nowhere is this more accurate than when applied to the Grand National. Not only has the race laid claim to drawing the largest live audience of any single sporting event, it also has a field that consistently totals 40.[1] The race, therefore, demands both appropriate spectacle and large-scale spaces. After concluding that its facilities were no longer perceived to be equal to these requisites, from 2005-7 the racecourse embarked upon a major redevelopment project. A pair of new viewing stands was built and, moreover, the parading experience was transformed.

Both phases were geared towards the delivery of that signature event, the Grand National. The stands were erected at a sharp corner of the track between the starting and finishing lines to best capture the excitement of these pivotal moments of the race. Meanwhile, a new parade ring was designed adjacent to them, and the old parade and weighing area was remodelled to create a new entrance, with the historic ring becoming a landscaped garden.

Not only was the new enclosure made bigger than its predecessor to safely accommodate the race's large field size, it was designed to rationalise the circulation of the horses from the stables to the corner of the track where the starting line is positioned. Prior to

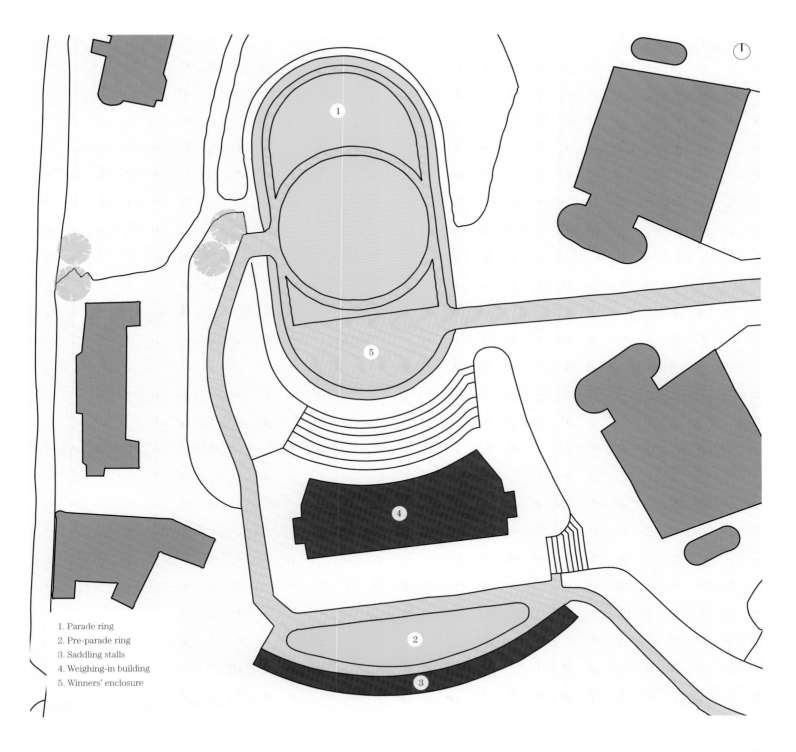

1. Parade ring
2. Pre-parade ring
3. Saddling stalls
4. Weighing-in building
5. Winners' enclosure

redevelopment, the horse route from the stables to the ring, and from the ring to the track doubled back on itself. The redevelopment simplified the processional path. From new stables to the south, horses now move to a shady pre-parade ring aligned on the axis of the parade ring. From here, they are led a final 100 metres (328 feet) between two steel fences beneath the arch of the new grandstands to the starting line.

The parade ring is no longer square in shape but an oval, with the winner's enclosure now installed at its centre. Exploiting the slight natural slope of the topography, it was conceived as an amphitheatre-like space to facilitate viewing. With a stepped terrace at its southern end and surrounding viewing slopes, it provided space for 3,000 racegoers. Its orientation was deliberately planned to capture the afternoon sun in early April when the Grand National is held, highlighting the triumphant horse and rider on their return procession from the track whilst also warming spectators in the chilly spring weather. Overlooking the ring from the south, a curved, two-storey building capped with a white tensile canopy was constructed. The lower floor was occupied by a media centre, while the upper storey housed a glass-fronted weighing room, from which the jockeys descend theatrically to the ring.[2]

Right: Modern-day aerial view, showing the extent of Aintree's 2005–7 redevelopment

Above: The parade ring in
1950 before the 104th running
of the Grand National. In
attendance are King George
VI and Queen Elizabeth in the
centre of the ring

Opposite: Aintree's
2005–7 redevelopment
eased and aggrandised
the parade procession

Arlington Park
Illinois, USA

When it was erected in 1927, Arlington Park was America's most modern racecourse. Reportedly costing $2 million, it comprised two tracks, stables for up to 2,700 horses, a steel-and-glass grandstand with seating for 16,000 and, directly behind this, a parade ring. It was a simple, turfed oval, encircled by white fencing to separate the public and dotted with newly planted trees. Along one side, perpendicular to the grandstand, ran a low range of covered saddling stalls. Its park-like ambience – only 50 kilometres (30 miles) northwest of the gritty, urban Chicago Loop – formed one of Arlington's primary attractions.

In 1960, the parade ring was reconfigured, set back parallel to and further from the rear of the grandstand. The by-now-mature trees provided a green canopy.

Today, this area looks very different. Indeed, since then, the whole track has been radically transformed for, in 1985, a disastrous fire rampaged through its grandstand. Illinois's most famous thoroughbred venue was reduced to a smouldering ruin. Out of its ashes, though, rose a remodelled Arlington, completed in 1989.

The new Arlington was smaller but more lavish than ever before – construction costs were estimated at anything between $125 million to $200 million. Its owner, Richard Duchossois, had high ambitions and a willingness to dig deep into his coffers to realise them. Thus, to complement the sleek new grandstand, in 1993 the paddock was also redesigned.

The parade ring sits closely behind the midpoint of the grandstand. Sixty per cent larger than its predecessor, the near-circular ring is bisected by a pathway around which four trees are symmetrically arranged. The saddling shed, crescent in plan, lies on its northern side. Open to the sides and front, the architecture of the shed speaks of a bygone age of racing. Colonial in style, it is a single-storey structure from which rise polygonal turrets at its midpoint and at either end. Internally, it is liberally outfitted in polished timber. On either side, the building is flanked by the jockeys' quarters and maintenance offices, making the paddock area a hive of activity.

The ring is undoubtedly designed to be at the heart of Arlington, and special attention has been paid to ensure good views for all. Balconies extend from every floor of the grandstand's rear façade while, at ground level, visibility is facilitated by the ring's sunken format. The almost-circular shape of the concave ring makes for a theatrical effect. It is surrounded by a shallow gallery fenced by white railings around which patrons gather to scrutinise Arlington's thoroughbred athletes as they emerge from the saddling stalls to begin their pre-race promenade.

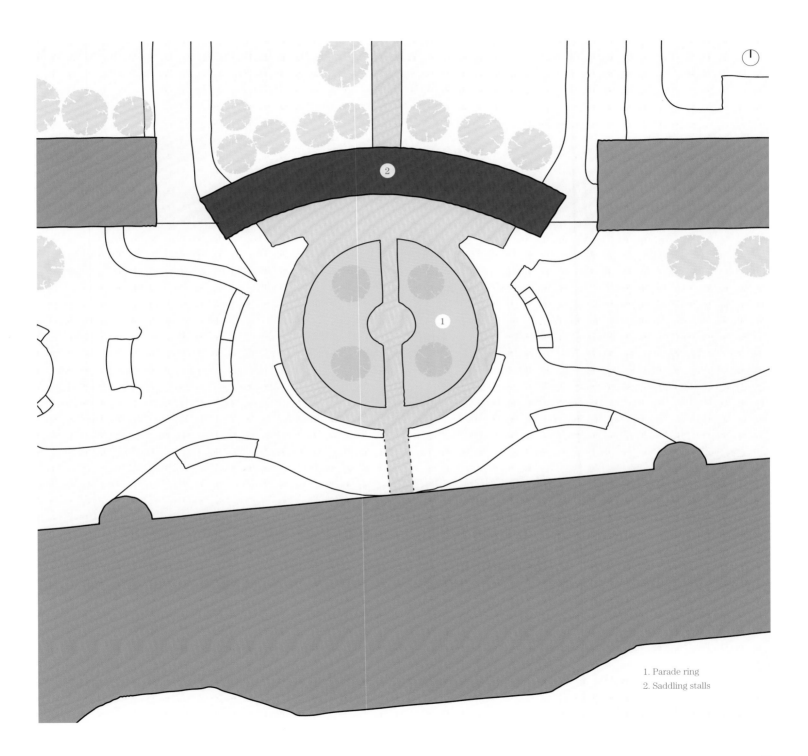

1. Parade ring
2. Saddling stalls

Above: Shown here in
1936, Arlington's original
parade ring was a simple,
tree-studded oval

Opposite: The ring was
redesigned in 1993 as
a near-circle with open
saddling stalls to the north

Ascot Racecourse
Berkshire, UK

Despite ranking as one of the world's most historic racecourses, Ascot boasts one of the UK's newest parade ring complexes. Unveiled in 2006, it was a key feature of a wholesale redevelopment which also saw the construction of a vast new grandstand and the restoration of Ascot's Victorian and Edwardian buildings. Today's parade ring is, though, but the latest chapter in a long history of saddling and parading enclosures at the storied track.

In the nineteenth century, Ascot – which had been founded in 1711 – was at the vanguard of a country-wide reform of pre-race procedure intended to systematise and hone the sport. In 1838, in time for its annual June races, it instituted a 'regulation that the horses in every race shall be saddled in front of [the new weighing stand]'.[3] However, the rule was more often broken than observed, even when, in 1845, it was ordained that saddling was to take place in the newly created enclosure in front of the Royal Box, which was entered only by Ascot's most privileged attendees.[4]

By 1863, Ascot's leadership had abandoned this saddling enclosure. 'For some years past it has been but too obvious that even the indulgence of those in authority has been unable to keep pace with the unscrupulous attempt of others to transgress it,' reported *Lloyd's Weekly Newspaper* on 17 May 1863.

The grass plot nominally called 'the saddling enclosure' will henceforth not only cease to be so-called, but actually to be used for any such purpose. The clerk of the course has been compelled to report the impossibility any longer properly to discharge his duties of weighing and taking entries, owing to the wholesale intrusion into this enclosure by persons who have neither right nor reason to intrude.

Instead, the following year, a designated saddling paddock was created at the western end of the viewing stands.

In the second half of the nineteenth century, it became common practice at British racecourses to delineate a paddock enclosure where patrons could mingle with the horsemen and horses during the pre- and post-race preparations. Ascot's new paddock (for those willing to pay the 10s entrance fee) was quickly established as the heart of the course and the subject of continual improvement works, beginning in 1878. That year, the saddling boxes that stood within it were demolished to make room for a 73-metre (240-feet) long range of stalls lining its southern side; in 1887, a state-of-the-art tunnel was constructed running 108 metres (350 feet) from the Grand Stand Lawn to the paddock enclosure, facilitating movement across the increasingly crowded grounds; and in 1902, following an extension to the paddock acreage, a weighing room, loose

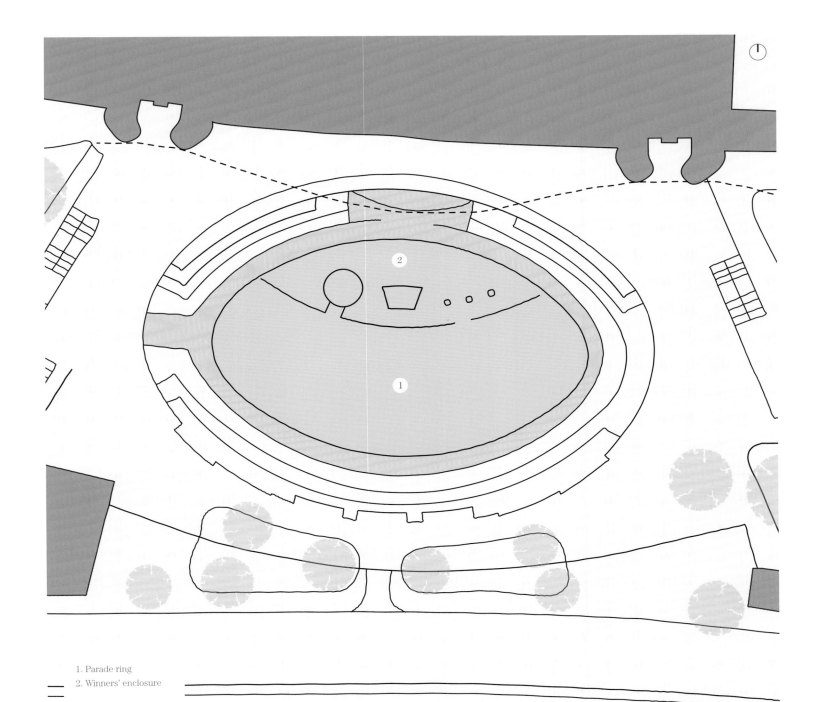

1. Parade ring
2. Winners' enclosure

boxes, doctor's rooms and a magistrate's court were erected around its southern and eastern perimeter.

In 1914, the area of the paddock was expanded once again enabling the realisation of a significant reordering of the enclosure. 'In the enlarged paddock,' reported *The Times* on 3 June 1914, 'two parade rings have been added, one a general exercise ring at the west end, the other, for the horses engaged in the race about to take place.' The western ring must rank as one of the earliest defined pre-parade rings. In 1929-30, the paddock's western boundary was extended further and saddling boxes erected along it, resulting in a commodious yet sheltered environment.

This layout survived until the 1960s. Between 1960 and 1964, the face of Ascot was transformed as its Victorian and Edwardian stands were replaced with a state-of-the-art grandstand and Royal Enclosure. The paddock too was remodelled. The parade ring was rearranged into the position it would occupy for the next forty years. Throughout this time, the paddock was a much-cherished area of the racecourse. It was championed as a rural idyll, its pastoral atmosphere characterised by the dappled light which shone through the canopy of ancient trees.

For all its sylvan charm, though, the location of the paddock was not well suited to the circulation of large attendances. With the main parade ring sited some 100 metres (328 feet) beyond the grandstand, patrons wishing to visit it were compelled to trudge along the narrow pedestrian passage alongside the track or through the busy Victorian tunnel which frequently required traffic lights to direct the crowds. By the turn of the century, on major race days, the two routes quickly became congested bottlenecks. Ascot's buildings too were cause for concern. With the stands and main facilities deteriorating and becoming increasingly difficult and costly to maintain, in 2003 the racecourse embarked upon a three-year redevelopment, which involved a new pre-parade ring and the relocation of the main parade ring to the geographical heart of the racecourse.

With Royal Ascot attracting daily audiences of up to 80,000, the key priorities of the new ring were size and accessibility. Sited immediately behind the new grandstand, it was an oval amphitheatre surrounded by high-banked concrete steps with an 8,000-capacity that offered an uninterrupted view of the horses and, of course, of the culminating stage of the royal procession. The winners' circle was moved from the front of the Royal Enclosure to a more visible position in the ring. Since 2011, the ring has had a new inhabitant in the form of an over-life-size bronze depicting one of Ascot's greatest past stars, the four-time Gold Cup winner Yeats.

The loss of the old, tree-shaded parade ring was lamented by many in 2006 when the redevelopment was unveiled. Yet few contest that the changes brought about a more accessible and egalitarian parade ring experience for the full spectrum of Ascot's racegoers.

Above: Ascot's parade ring was remodelled and enlarged in the 1960s following a wholesale redevelopment of the course

Opposite: Today's parade ring, as viewed from the grandstand, is the product of Ascot's latest redevelopment (2003-6)

Belmont Park
New York, USA

Upon its opening in 1905, Belmont's saddling paddock was eulogised as 'the most beautiful seen anywhere in this country'.[5] The paddock was a vast lawn, studded with trees, extending behind the grandstand. Throughout its construction, Belmont's owners were meticulous in their dedication to preserving the trees already standing on the land and to planting more.

Although only 34 kilometres (21 miles) from Manhattan, Belmont immediately gained a reputation as a 'bucolic beauty'. Horses, horsemen and patrons circulated freely as the thoroughbreds were saddled and exercised beneath the trees. Benches in the paddock provided seating for 1,000 racegoers. On rainy days, saddling took place under the shelter of a large timber shed sited immediately to the rear of the clubhouse and grandstand. Measuring 90 by 25 metres (295 by 83 feet), it housed 36 stalls. It no longer survives, but its form corresponded to the saddling shed that still stands at Saratoga Race Course built only three years earlier.

The landmark of the paddock was a tall white pine. Said to be over a century old when Belmont opened, patrons sat under its comforting shade upon benches which encircled it. Although today Belmont's paddock looks very different to its 1905 opening day, this stately old pine still stands sentry at its centre.

Belmont's paddock is now an oval enclosure framed by a curved saddling shed and tiered, amphitheatre-style steps which provide a clear view over the parade ring. The arrangement dates from the racecourse's 1963-8 redevelopment. Notwithstanding that this saw a complete rebuilding of the complex, the ambience of old Belmont Park was scrupulously preserved, most notably in the safeguarding of its tree canopy. The shape of the walking circle was expanded at one end to accommodate the white pine, now majestically gnarled and supported by wires and braces. Benches still encircle its base, around which ivy creeps.

White ironwork encloses the walking ring, complete with ornamental equestrian scenes of jockeys and horses around the viewing gallery that were conserved from pre-1963. The crescent saddling stalls are roofed but open to both sides; members of the public can walk behind the shed to survey the pre-race preparation, whilst its front aspect can be seen by owners and the media with the privilege of entering the restricted area within the ring. And from its centre, Belmont's (arguably) most celebrated past champion of all looks on. A bronze statue of Secretariat, the 1973 Triple Crown winner, depicted at full gallop surveys Belmont's current hopefuls as they promenade around the tree-shaded ring.

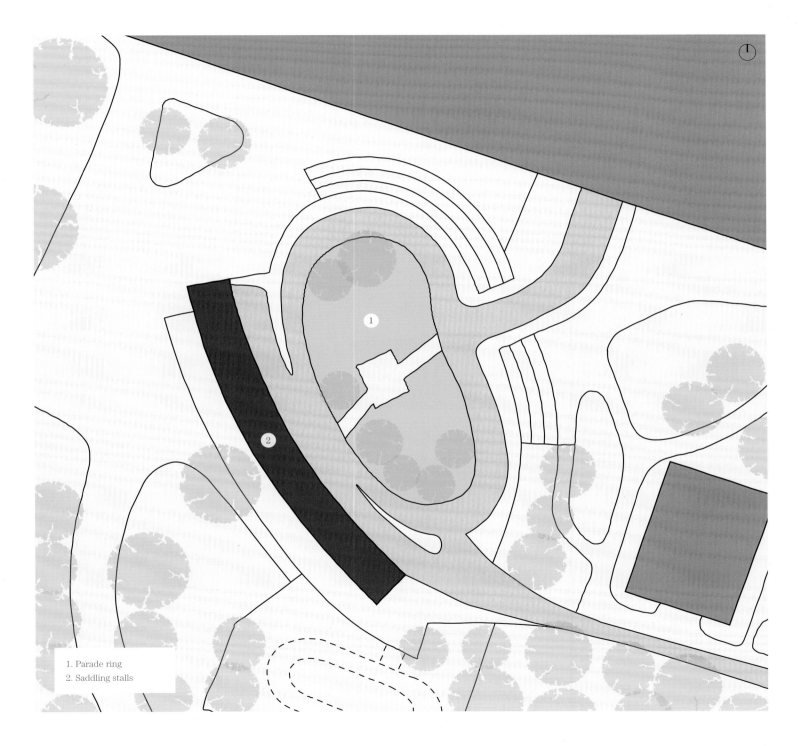

1. Parade ring
2. Saddling stalls

49

Above: The saddling shed
at the heart of the paddock,
photographed in 1905 upon
Belmont Park's opening, where
the equine athletes were
saddled on rainy days

Opposite: Today's parade
ring is presided over by a
bronze of Belmont hero,
Secretariat. Behind are
the saddling stalls

SECRETARIAT

MEADOW STABLE'S CHESTNUT COLT, 1970
BY BOLD RULER OUT OF SOMETHINGROYAL BY PRINCEQUILLO
HORSE OF THE YEAR IN 1972 AND 1973
WINNER OF THE TRIPLE CROWN IN 1973

BRED BY MEADOW STUD, INC., DOSWELL, VIRGINIA
TRAINED BY LUCIEN LAURIN · RIDDEN BY RON TURCOTTE

JOHN SKEAPING, R.A. SCULPTOR, 1974
GIFT OF PAUL MELLON TO THE NATIONAL MUSEUM OF RACING AT SARATOGA

Churchill Downs
Kentucky, USA

Horseracing has flourished in Kentucky since the 1780s. And following its opening day on 17 May 1875 – also the first running of the Kentucky Derby – Churchill Downs has been its spiritual home. The twin spires of its 1895 grandstand remain the image ever associated with the physical realm of the racecourse, but the parade ring occupies a central place within its environment.

The area reserved for the exercising and saddling of horses at Churchill Downs has had a peripatetic history. By the early twentieth century, it was sited behind the northern end of the extended grandstand; in 1924, a larger paddock was constructed as the centre of activity behind the 1895 grandstand and an 5.5-metre- (18-feet) wide horse-walk leading from it was created between the old stand and newly improved clubhouse; in 1941, it was moved again, 21 metres (70 feet) northwards to improve public viewing of the pre-race exercising.

By the running of the 113th Kentucky Derby in 1987, the area had been remodelled once more. Hitherto, the saddling of the horses had taken place in a dark building shaded by a low roof tucked under the superstructure of the grandstand, too small to comfortably accommodate a 20-horse Derby field or the throng of groomsmen, reporters and television crews. The redevelopment enhanced the saddling experience, making it more visible and commodious, and returned it to the centre of the action. It invested Churchill Downs with a larger, airier saddling shed, containing 20 stalls and spanning 67 metres (220 feet) in length built on a site formerly used as parking for television-support trucks. Long and thin in shape, it bounded the northern edge of a new oval parade ring, measuring 21 by 55 metres (70 by 180 feet). Located to the rear of the 1895 grandstand with its centrepoint aligned to the axis of the building's easternmost spire, the new walking ring was repositioned on much the same spot as its 1924 predecessor.

This is the parade ring that greets racegoers to Churchill Downs today. Upgrades have been undertaken in the intervening years – notably to the surfaces of the stalls and ring, which are now a slip-resistant, shock-absorbing rubber, and to the display boards above the stalls. The interior of the ring has horseshoe-shaped parterres, and it is enclosed by white-rail fencing against which racing fans press to catch a glimpse of future Derby winners.

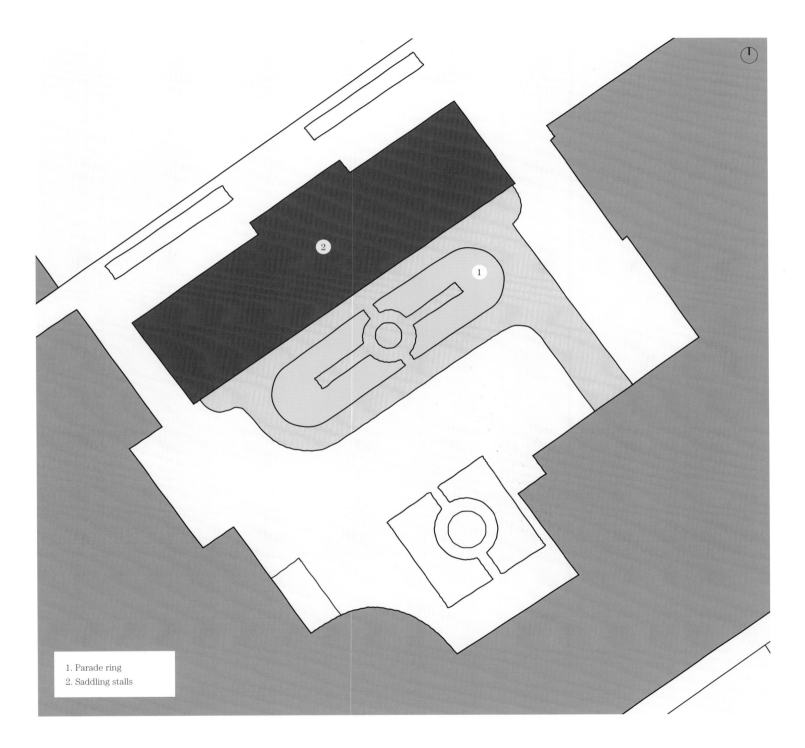

1. Parade ring
2. Saddling stalls

Above: The roofed
saddling shed, circa 1920,
within the paddock

Opposite: The paddock on Derby
day. As the celebrated home of the
Kentucky Derby, the parade ring
must accommodate a 20-horse
field size, a media bevy and
enormous crowds of racegoers

Club Hipico de Santiago
Santiago, Chile

Chile's oldest racecourse is a physical expression of the golden era of thoroughbred racing in South America in the early decades of the twentieth century. The Club Hipico de Santiago had been founded in 1869, but in 1918 it began a wholesale remodelling of its course and all its buildings. By the mid-1920s, the racecourse had been transformed into, arguably, the most imaginative, lavish and beautiful example of its age anywhere in the world, featuring an architecturally eclectic collection of grandstands, stables, gardens, club house and even a musicians' pavilion. The present-day parade ring also belongs to this ensemble.

The parade ring was an integral component of the grand redevelopment. Spanning approximately 60 metres (197 feet) in length, it was sited behind the vast Members' Stand, and typified the historicist persona of the racecourse's new buildings. The Members' Stand was Parisian in style, the two public stands were inspired by Quattrocento Italy, the musicians' pavilion sported a Grecian aesthetic, and the parade ring was given a Mission Revival flavour, inspired by eighteenth-century Spanish Franciscan churches of the southwest US.

Saddling stalls were located at the western end of the oval arena, built with round arched openings, low-pitched red-tile roofs, white-stucco walls, plus a bell tower-like structure at their centre. On either side of the paddock, office and jockey buildings continued this Mission Revival theme. Here, the round arched windows, heavy wooden doors, overhanging eaves, and intricately carved wooden trim which typified Mission architecture were fused with flourishes of Baroque swags and cornucopias applied to their stucco surfaces. The whole ensemble makes for one of the most picturesque parade rings in the whole of racing.[6]

In the intervening years since its completion in 1919, the parade ring has changed little in its character but has nonetheless seen some alterations in its organisation. For example, the white picket fence that enclosed the original ring was replaced by low metal railings emblazoned with the club's monogram. In 2009, it underwent more prominent remodelling. The walking surface was replaced, and a viewing pergola (not part of the original scheme), which had hitherto bisected the ring was removed, enabling the two lawned walking circles within the ring to be enlarged. By giving more space for the parade of the horses, the modifications brought added appeal to Santiago's ring.

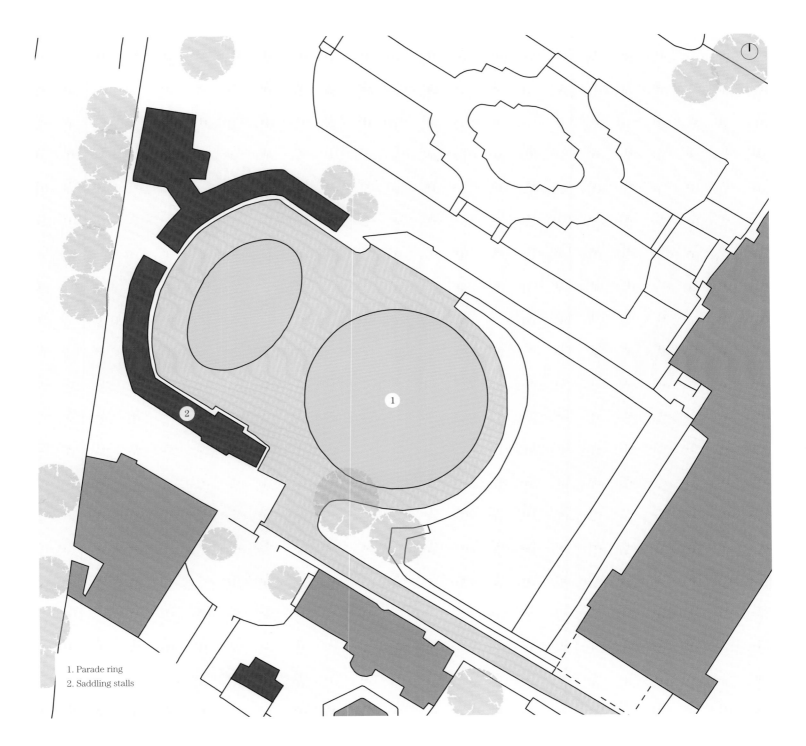

1. Parade ring
2. Saddling stalls

Above: Although founded in 1869, a wholesale redevelopment from 1918-24 transformed the course into a showpiece of exuberant landscaping and architecture

Opposite: Remodelled in 2009, the parade ring is still characterised by the Mission Revival spirit of its saddling stalls and surrounding structures

Del Mar Turf Club
California, USA

The Del Mar Turf Club opened in 1937, run by a showbusiness consortium with members including Bing Crosby and Paramount Studios acting as corporate sponsor, as part of a fairground complex. The aura of glamour provided by Crosby and pals, combined with the charm of its architecture made Del Mar unique.

The Turf Club was designed as a tribute to California's Spanish missionary history. It was envisioned as a city in miniature in which Mission Revival architecture – characterised by stucco-sheathed walls, rounded arch windows, and low-pitched clay-tile roofs – was used to create an ambiance of Spanish romance.

The paddock was imagined as the main plaza of a pueblo, and was often lauded as the most intimate part of the racecourse complex. It consisted of a circular walking ring framed by a wooden cross fence, bounded on two sides by a range of saddling stalls and the clubhouse. Described by one commentator as 'the most romantic saddling shed found in any of America's racetracks', the saddling enclosure had dirt floors, adobe walls and a roof clad in bark-stripped logs upheld by sturdy wooden posts.[7] Over time, climbing ivy covered its façade.

For over half a century, the paddock served as the site of Del Mar's pre-race saddling and parading ritual. However, in 1991 the Turf Club embarked upon an $80-million redevelopment, which saw the original grandstand and clubhouse replaced and the parade ring transformed. The overhaul was unveiled in 1993.

The ring is now oval in shape, larger in size, and encircled by a low, green hedge. It is sited further westwards than its predecessor in a more central location, overlooked by the new grandstand's verandas. Echoes of the 1937 paddock remain, however. One side of the ring is lined by a range of saddling stalls, whose ivy-clad arches and red clay-tile roofs pay homage to Del Mar's Mission Revival heritage. On the opposite side, patrons can watch the ceremonial parade from shallow tiered steps divided by the horse walk, which leads through the grandstand via a cathedral-like entrance to the track. Perhaps the new Del Mar lacks some of the charm of the original, yet its paddock wants none of the charisma that has been associated with the seaside course since its earliest, star-filled days.

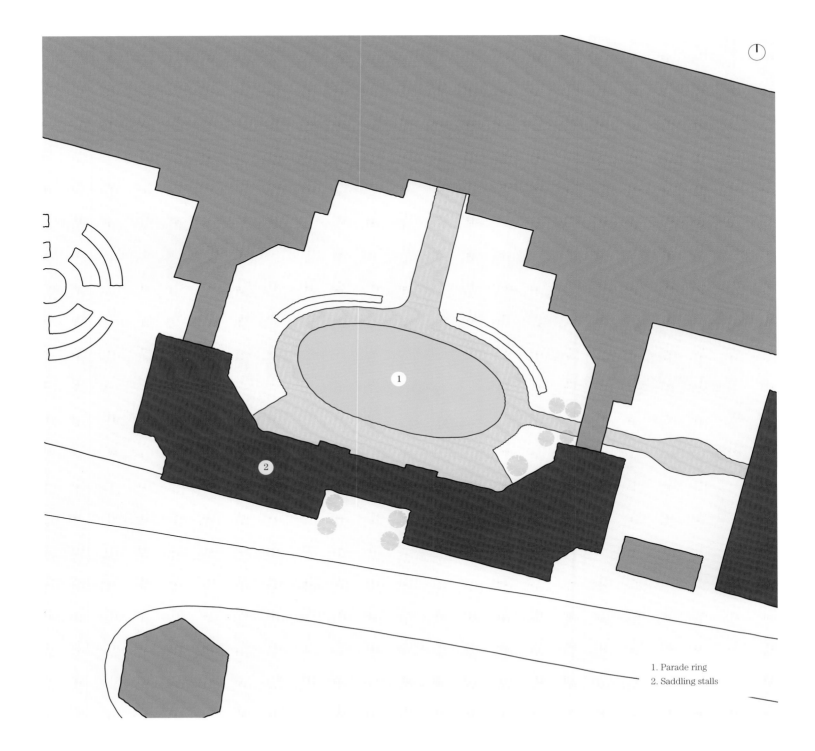

1. Parade ring
2. Saddling stalls

Above: Built in 1937, Del Mar's parade ring stood behind its glamorous Mission Revival stands

Opposite: Although rebuilt in 1993, Del Mar's buildings and parade ring are still imbued with a Spanish Mission aura

Flemington Racecourse
Melbourne, Australia

In the decades following its first race meeting in 1810, Australia embraced thoroughbred racing on a singular scale. The national enthusiasm for the sport is encapsulated by 'The Race that Stops a Nation' – the Melbourne Cup – held at Flemington Racecourse since its first running in 1861. While its global fame is firmly entwined with that one event, the racecourse in fact predates it by 20 years.

In 1840, racing at Flemington was inaugurated on a tract of open but flood-prone land, northwest of Melbourne's city centre. Few, if any, amenities were afforded. This typified the nature of early Australian racing. Most tracks were humble affairs, limited to an open field with posts roughly marking the racing circuit and wagons acting as grandstands. The 1860s, though, saw growing ambitions.

This was the height of the gold rush, and prospectors flocked to racecourses to enjoy their new-found riches. Racing in Australia flourished from a rustic entertainment into a prospering industry. In Melbourne, profits from the 1859 Australian Champions Sweepstakes provided Flemington's trustees with the means and resolve to transform the course.

In 1860, the track was reconfigured, a viewing stand was erected, and a saddling paddock was laid out to the west of the new building. Lying next to the Maribyrnong River and shaded by young trees, the paddock was a pastoral setting for the preparation of the horses and the perambulation of the spectators.

The 1880s were a boom time for Flemington. The racecourse underwent almost continuous aggrandisement with new public stands, tea pagoda, Swiss House and more. In 1887, the paddock too was remodelled to create what was christened the 'birdcage', an area set aside from the hustle of the rest of the course. 'For several years back trainers have had a serious ground for complaint in the manner in which they are hampered by the crowd in preparing the toilette of their equine charge,' recorded the *Illustrated Australian News* in November of that year. 'The V.R.C. [Victoria Racing Club] executive therefore determined to portion off a part of the saddling paddock with a high wire fence, and reserve it for the use of trainers and jockeys, the outside public being only admitted on the payment of 5s extra.' While some contemporaries pilloried this additional charge, others welcomed it as 'a great convenience to trainers and owners, in as much as it gave them greater facilities for bringing their charges to the post without being subject to the petty annoyances inseparable from the congregation of large crowds in the vicinity of the horses while saddling up'.[8] New planting and horse stalls completed the ensemble.

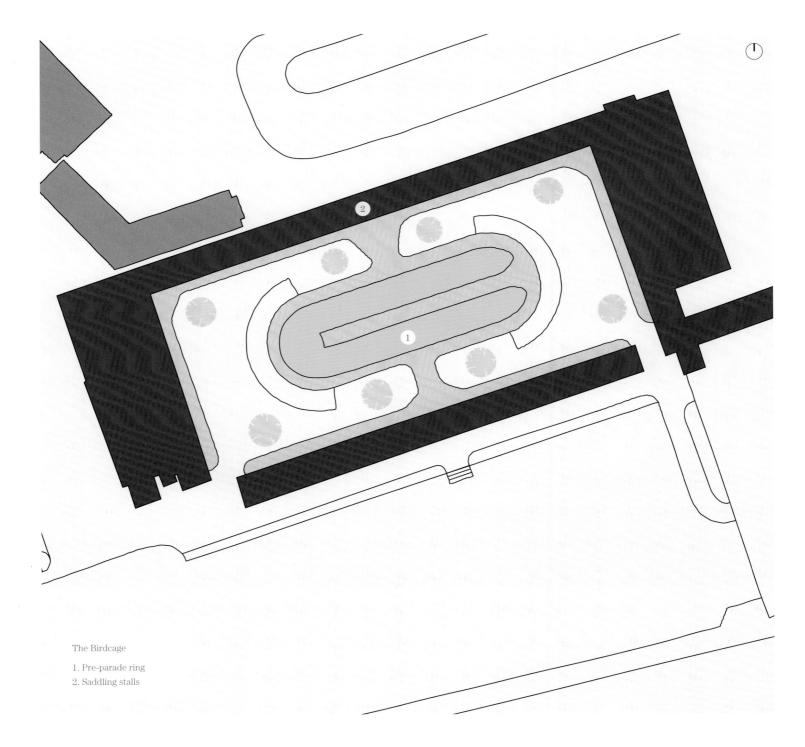

The Birdcage

1. Pre-parade ring
2. Saddling stalls

Above: Flemington's
pre-parade ring – or
birdcage – was relocated
to the eastern end of
the racecourse reserve
in 1924

Opposite: Today's birdcage has
remained in roughly the same
position since the 1920s, but now
has the sophisticated addition of
a tunnel leading directly to the
parade ring, or mounting yard

The 'birdcage' epithet was borrowed from the saddling paddock at Newmarket, although its actual connotations are disputed. According to some accounts, it stemmed from the fact that it was a place where elegant female patrons were on display just as much as the horses. Whatever its etymology, the area comprising Flemington's saddling stalls and pre-parade ring has been known as the birdcage ever since.

Various improvements and expansions were made to the paddock in subsequent years, but in the 1920s it was completely transformed. This decade saw dramatic changes at Flemington. Unprecedentedly high visitor numbers were causing overcrowding and congestion. However, the existing layout of the stands and the paddock next to the river at the western end of the site offered little scope for expansion. Radical changes were needed. Between 1922 and 1924, the racecourse made the bold move to shift the nucleus of its facilities to the east, to the empty flat land which had housed a carriage paddock. The redevelopment saw the construction of a new Members' Stand with a betting ring at its rear and a rectangular mounting yard in front. Beyond this, at the northeastern boundary of the racecourse reserve, new birdcage stalls, a Trainers' and Jockeys' Stand, and pre-parade ring were constructed. The latter was a spacious oval with a fountain at its centre.

Those who were attached to the atmosphere of the old Flemington, where the horses jostled amongst onlookers under the shelter of the mature fir, oak and elm trees, mourned the changes. Nonetheless, they undoubtedly improved the visibility of horses parading both in the birdcage exercise ring and in the mounting yard. The new layout brought with it a new, staged sequence of horse movement on race days, with an emphasis placed on theatrical display. The thoroughbreds progressed from the stalls, to the walking ring, then along an open pathway past the length of the new Members' Stand, and into the mounting yard where they would arrive ready for their jockeys and the race. The mounting yard, overlooked by the Members' Stand balconies, was reserved for officials, trainers, jockeys and owners. This routine has remained undisturbed since the 1920s, although the rings themselves have undergone alterations.

In 2007, the birdcage underwent a major remodelling. The ageing stalls, Trainers' and Jockeys' Stand, and ring were demolished, and a new complex of pre-parade ring and stalls opened, with the capacity to stable 125 horses for the length of the race day. The scheme also introduced a novel feature – a tunnel measuring some 180 metres (600 feet) leading from the new exercise ring, under the public lawn and emerging at the mounting yard in front of the Members' Stand. Year-on-year increases in attendances, particularly during Cup week, meant that horses had had to grapple against pressing crowds as they made their way along the narrow passage leading from the exercise ring to the mounting yard. The new tunnel diverted horses away from spectators, thereby improving safety and the flow of pedestrian traffic. The birdcage is now a hub of hospitality during the celebrated Melbourne Cup, when the lawned pre-parade ring is surrounded by elevated marquees.

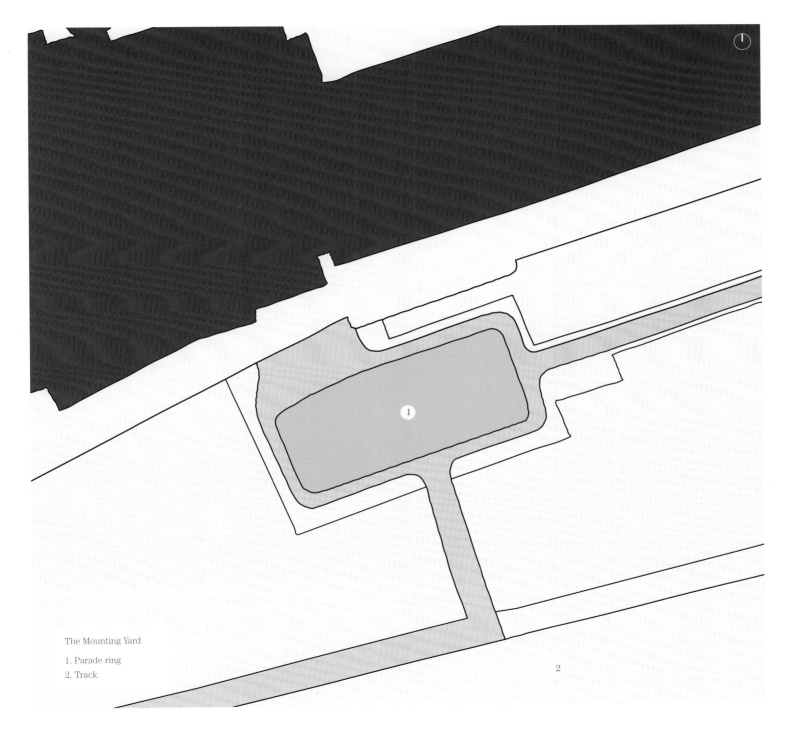

The Mounting Yard

1. Parade ring
2. Track

Above: When a new Members' Stand was built in 1924, a parade ring – or mounting yard – was installed in front of it

Opposite: Flemington's mounting yard has changed but little since the 1920s. Locating the ring in front of the stands is common practice in Australia and New Zealand but rarer elsewhere

Goodwood Racecourse
Sussex, UK

Goodwood is the birthplace of the parade ritual. It was here in the 1830s that Lord George Bentinck pioneered the introduction of a pre-race parade. It is only fitting, then, that today the racecourse boasts one of the most atmospheric and well-designed parade rings in thoroughbred racing.

As at many other racecourses, Goodwood's parade ring is a product of evolution. The paddock was originally sited alongside the track at the extreme western end of the course. By 1927, two fenced walking rings had been constructed within it. Goodwood's increasing popularity throughout the twentieth century made this location progressively impractical, however. By the 1950s, the summer festival drew a daily average of 50,000 racegoers. The crowds, combined with the paddock's position, meant, as one commentator recorded, 'that racegoers in Tattersalls had a Sabbath day's journey to reach it'.[9]

In 1976, this shortcoming was addressed. The parade and pre-parade rings and weighing room were relocated to the south side of the racecourse at the rear of the main stand, where they are still sited. Recent years have seen a tendency to relocate parade rings to more 'spectator-friendly' locations directly behind grandstands, such as occurred at Ascot in 2006 and Chantilly in 2007; but, in 1976, Goodwood was very much at the vanguard of that trend.

Nonetheless, by the late 1990s concerns were mounting that Goodwood was beginning to fall behind its competitors in terms of customer experience. Plans were launched to upgrade the quality of its facilities, and in 2001 a new winners' enclosure, weighing-in building and parade ring were opened.

The new design took advantage of the natural slope of the land to create an amphitheatre, surrounded by tiers of spectator steps bounded by neatly-clipped box hedge. It created space for 5,000 spectators, 2,000 more than its predecessor. The steps, made using the local building material of flint, extend from the side walls of the sunken weighing-in building. Built into the retaining wall of the parade ring, the weighing-in building is almost invisible. Its single-aspect elevation is fully glazed to overlook the winners' enclosure and parade ring beyond.[10] To the south, the pre-parade ring was rebuilt enclosed on its southern perimeter with stalls.

The most distinctive element of the ensemble is the three hospitality pavilions around the ring's perimeter. Housing bars and serveries beneath white masted canopies, the pavilions are essentially updated versions of the village-green marquee so enduringly associated with summer sports in Britain. Two of the pavilions are sheltered from the southerly winds with free-standing glass screens, but the principle of their design is to include as little structure as possible to ensure unimpeded views over the parade ring and to augment Goodwood's celebrated 'garden party' atmosphere.

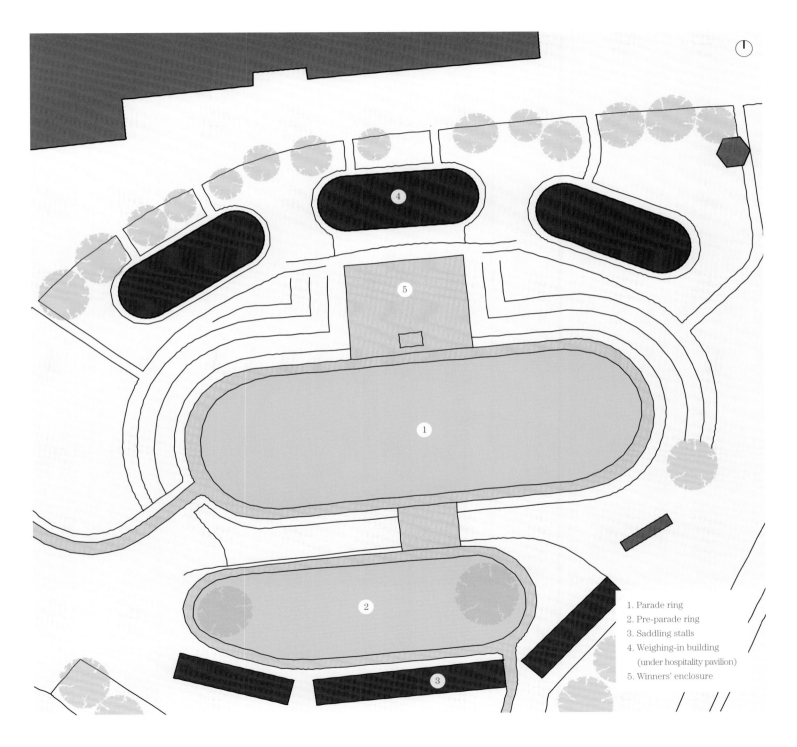

1. Parade ring
2. Pre-parade ring
3. Saddling stalls
4. Weighing-in building
   (under hospitality pavilion)
5. Winners' enclosure

Above: Goodwood in the 1920s.
The parade ring (foreground)
and pre-parade ring overlooked
by crowds thronging the Trundle
hill, racing's 'most glorious free
grandstand'

Opposite: Today's parade
ring dates from 2001,
surrounded by tiers of
spectator steps, weighing
room, winners' enclosure
and hospitality pavilions

Hippodrome de Chantilly
Picardy, France

The Hippodrome de Chantilly has been hosting racing since the sport was in its infancy in France. The country's oldest extant racecourse, it was founded in 1834 and by 1847 was popular enough to merit the construction of a set-piece ensemble of stands. The saddling paddock was a planned aspect of this early scheme. Situated to the rear of the stands, it was a semi-circular space bounded on its curved edge by stalls, a stewards' room, weighing room, and covered gallery. Here, patrons mingled unrestricted amongst the horses as they were saddled.

As the nineteenth century advanced, thoroughbred racing in France progressed in strides and by 1879 Chantilly had outgrown its original buildings. A new range of larger, grander stands comprising a *Grande Tribune* for the public and a *Tribune du Comité* was completed in 1881, and with them a new paddock was created. It was relocated away from the rear of the stands to the west of the *Tribune du Comité*, parallel to the track. In 1911, a weighing pavilion was built alongside it.

By the late twentieth century, however, this elongated layout was proving inefficient in terms of the circulation of Chantilly's crowds. The trek to and from the paddock (by this time with an enclosed parade ring) was an inconveniently long one for racegoers, who were compressed along the finishing straight. By the turn of the following century, grand modernisation plans were afoot. In 2007, as the second phase of a two-part redevelopment, the hippodrome unveiled a new parade ring and weighing room. This is the ring that greets patrons today.

During the redevelopment, special permission was secured to realign the road running behind the grandstand, pushing it back into the Forest of Chantilly behind. This created the space for the ring to be laid out behind the stand, echoing the placement of the 1847 paddock. In other respects, however, the new ring is very different from the informality of the original version. It is a formal walking ring, bounded by white fencing, and sunken to facilitate viewing. Patrons stand on the three tiers of shallow steps which encircle the space to watch the parading ritual. It has an unusual kidney-bean outline, a shape which reflects the semi-circular projection on the grandstand's rear façade. On its western perimeter, stands the weighing room, complete with rooftop terrace and clad with the same stone employed by the neighbouring 1881 grandstand.

Since its opening, the parade ring has proven an unmitigated success. It immediately improved circulation, whilst maintaining the celebrated charm of Chantilly's picturesque environment.

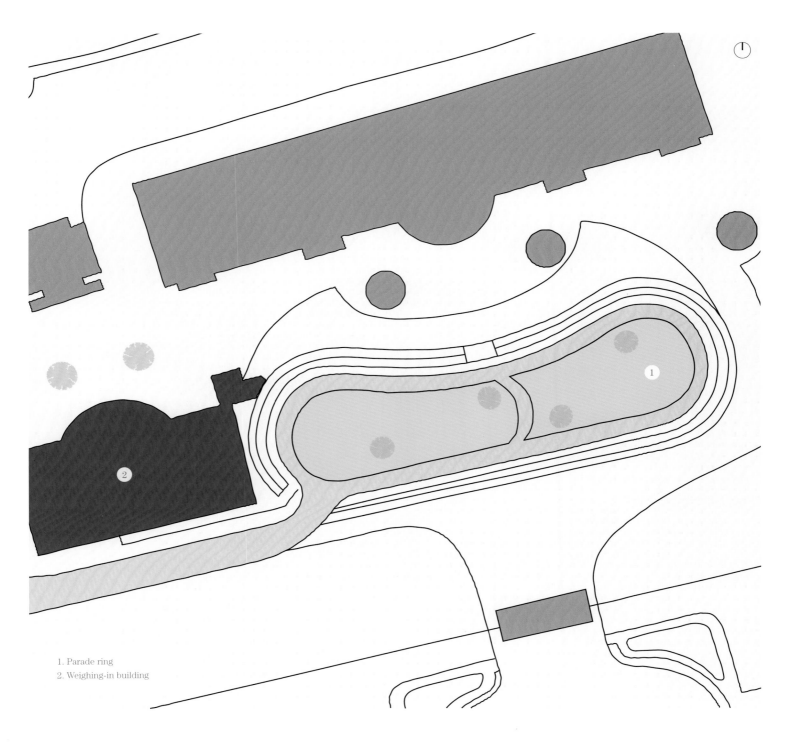

1. Parade ring
2. Weighing-in building

Above: Chantilly's first
paddock, shown here
in an 1852 illustration,
where horses, patrons
and jockeys mingled
informally

Opposite: Chantilly's
parade ring was relocated
back to its original
position to the rear of the
grandstand in 2007

Hippodrome de Longchamp
Paris, France

Napoleon III once asserted that he began to learn how to govern an empire 'from his intercourse with the calm, self-possessed men of the English turf'.[11] It is unsurprising then that when, in 1856, he was approached for permission to lay out a racecourse in Paris's newly created Bois de Boulogne, he readily gave consent. Following its inauguration in 1857, Longchamp – as the new racecourse was christened after the abbey that had once stood on its site – quickly flourished. Its races became the centre of a social whirl of balls, promenades and parties for the Parisian elite, aided by its easily accessible location on the outskirts of the city and, furthermore, by the grandeur of its physical environment.

The racecourse consisted of an ensemble of five stands, stretching 250 metres (820 feet) in length and hosting nearly 5,000 spectators. As typified racecourses of that period, it had no designated parade ring, but horses were saddled and walked in the vast garden between the entrance gate and the stands.

Succeeding decades saw enlargements and improvements to Longchamp's physical fabric, but none so dramatic as the redevelopment which took place between 1962-7. Driven by the need to compete with new racecourses built in the US and South America, as well as wholesale refurbishments such as that which had taken place at Ascot and The Curragh, Longchamp saw the phased replacement of its grandstands, weighing room, stalls and parade ring.

The new parade ring opened in April 1964. It was designed both to improve the safety of the passage of horses and to increase spectator capacity. The large new ring created an amphitheatre space for watching the parading pageant. It was surrounded not only by tall, tiered steppings, but also elevated terraces extending from the rear of the grandstands. This created a spacious arena with room for 5,000 racegoers. Alongside, an intimate pre-parade ring area was developed consisting of three small walking ovals lying shoulder to shoulder and enclosed by stalls. As is often the case in France, it is not designed for public access.[12]

For over 50 years, the parade ring has served the racecourse. It makes for one of the Turf's most atmospheric rings, especially on large race days such as the Prix de l'Arc de Triomphe when crowds press to get close to the white railings. Its leafy canopy of mature plane trees has shaded countless champions. Now, though, it is scheduled to be replaced. In 2011, designs were unveiled for a comprehensive remodelling of the historic racecourse. The 1960s grandstands are set to be superseded by a single, large structure, and the site of the ring is to be moved northwards to sit behind the new stand. The plans have been the subject of debate and delays, but, as the schedule currently stands, visitors to Longchamp in 2017 will encounter a brand new parade ring.

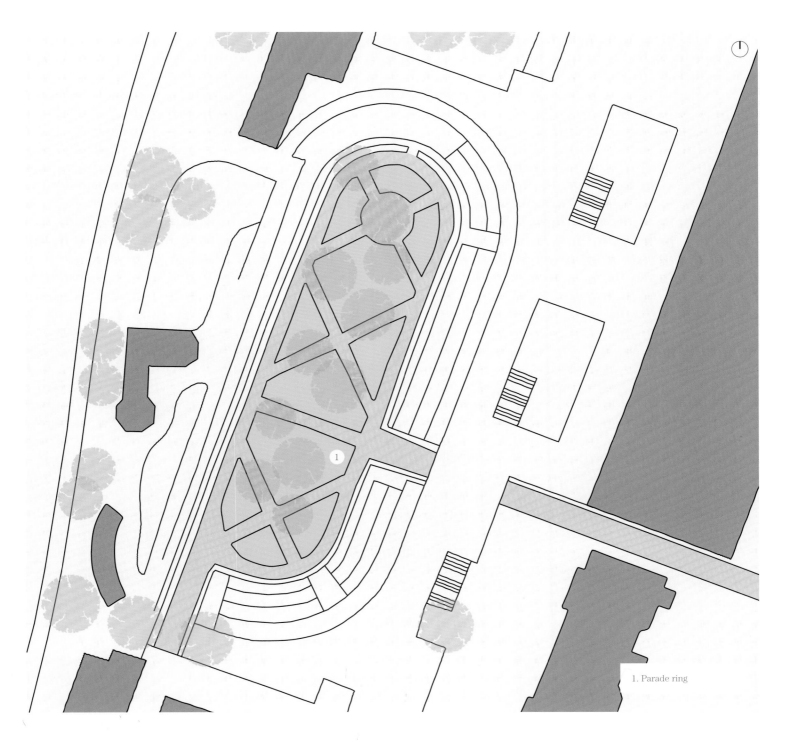

1. Parade ring

Above: *Le paddock de Longchamp en 1857*. In the nineteenth century, saddling and mounting was an unceremonious process, taking place amidst watching racegoers

Opposite: The intimate, tree-lined atmosphere of today's parade ring, which was installed in the 1960s

Keeneland Race Course
Kentucky, USA

There are few places in the world more closely associated with the thoroughbred than the rolling hills of the Bluegrass Region and its fulcrum city, Lexington. Recorded races began there as early as 1787, only 12 years after it was settled. Yet, in 1933, racing in Lexington came to an abrupt halt. Since 1826, meetings had been held at the Kentucky Association racecourse but decades of financial struggles and physical decline finally forced its permanent closure in the spring of that year. Fortunately for Lexington, a forward-thinking committee of local turfites quickly began the search for a replacement venue. Out of a potential 20 locations, these men selected the site which would become Keeneland.

From the outset, the committee determined that Keeneland was to be a new kind of course. It was envisioned as a 'model racetrack dedicated solely to the perpetuation and improvement of the sport and specifically committed never to seek profits'.[13] Thoroughbred racing was to be showcased at its best and all earnings were to be used for purses, capital facilities and local charities.[14] Since Keeneland's opening day on 15 October 1936, this ethos has been upheld. And it has been reflected in its unique physical environment.

Amongst the most notable features of its buildings and landscape is the paddock. Bordered by a low hedge to the west, limestone wall to the east and, at its northern end, a curving row of limestone saddling stalls, Keeneland's paddock is an intimate, park-like space situated directly behind the grandstand. It began life looking very different, however.

Keeneland Race Course was built on the half-completed shell of a private training and racing club, which had been owned by dedicated turfman Jack Keene. In 1916, Keene began building his dream track – a place devoted to the advancement of the horse industry and the thoroughbred stock in Kentucky. It was to be constructed to the highest architectural quality, united by a limestone palette quarried from his own farm. His ambitions, though, were never fully realised. After spending nearly 20 years and some $400,000, in 1935 the impoverished Keene was forced to sell the unfinished complex to the committee that would become the Keeneland Association.[15]

Keene's club had been built as a very personal labour of love and, as such, its design included several idiosyncratic elements. Not least of these was an indoor training track, measuring 400 metres (one quarter of a mile) in circumference and incorporating 48 horse stalls. When the Keeneland Association purchased the

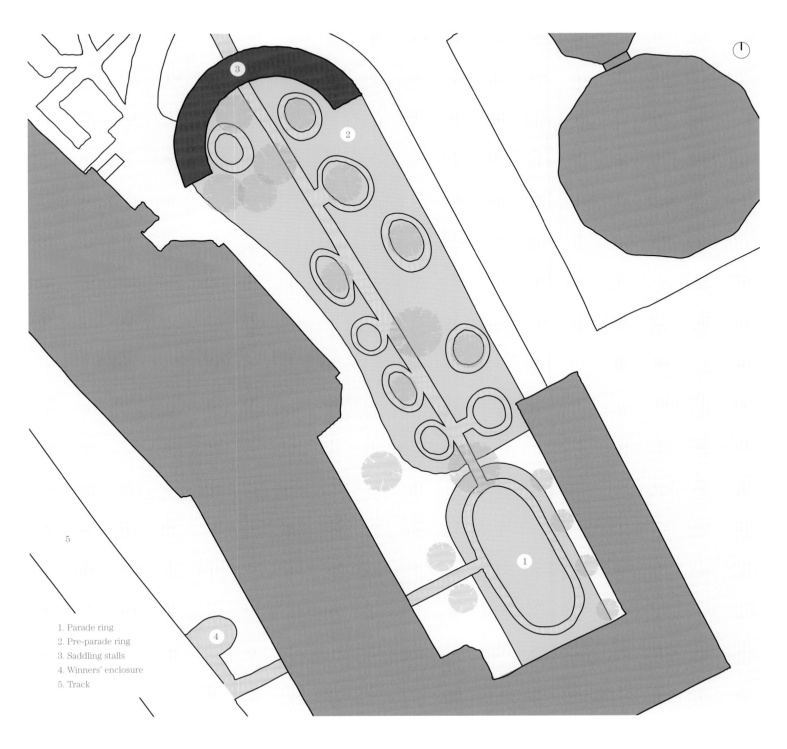

1. Parade ring
2. Pre-parade ring
3. Saddling stalls
4. Winners' enclosure
5. Track

91

site, this singular structure was deemed surplus to requirements but, with a waste-not-want-not outlook befitting the Association's limited resources, it was decided that it could be repurposed. Much to Keene's despair – he wept as he looked on – its limestone walls were knocked down to chest height, its interior walls were dynamited, and an outdoor saddling paddock was thereby created. Horses were saddled at the northern end, while a white-fenced walking ring was established to the south. Enclosed stalls along one side provided saddling space during inclement weather.[16]

While, since that time, Keeneland's physical estate has expanded in reflection of its growing success, the paddock still occupies the same spot. The legacy of its unorthodox genesis continues to be reflected in its form today, and, indeed, has resulted in several features which distinguishes it from the mainstream of parade ring design in North America. Firstly, it is in unusually close proximity to the grandstand-clubhouse complex which stretches along its western length. Through the large glazed windows and spacious balconies that span the building's rear façade, racegoers are afforded excellent views of the pre-race ritual.

Secondly, Keeneland continues to have a separate saddling area and walking ring, which approximates much closer to the UK template of separate pre-parade and parade rings than the US norm. Unusual

by British standards, though, the saddling enclosure is much larger than the parade ring.

The saddling area is bucolic in its atmosphere. Keeneland is famed for its commitment to landscape. Aristocratic pear trees line its track rail, Autumn Blaze maples frame its driveway, files of pin oaks fill its car park; and the paddock follows suit. The saddling enclosure is spotted by a miscellany of trees, including sugar maple, dogwood, crab apple, linden, and white pine, many of which are encircled by individual walking rings. The rings, like Keeneland's other horse paths, are made from rubberised bricks recycled from old tyres that provide a secure footing for the thoroughbreds. At its northern end, it is framed by a semi-circle of 16 saddling stalls. Added in 1984, the limestone fabric of the stalls blends seamlessly with the earlier architecture of the neighbouring grandstand and clubhouse.

Once saddled, horses momentarily cross through the crowd to make the brief journey to the oval parade ring. It is presided over by a towering white sycamore believed to have been planted at the time of Keeneland's opening. With no tiered viewing steppings or equivalent, the throng of racegoers that typically surrounds the parade ring often hampers sightlines, and yet the paddock is cherished as an embodiment of the relaxed, pastoral spirit for which Keeneland is renowned.

KEENELAND

Above: Photographed circa 1948, the walking ring is shown clearly delineated within the wider expanse of the tree-studded paddock

Opposite: The formal parade ring (foreground) and, behind, the saddling area dominated by a majestic white-barked sycamore

94

Newmarket Racecourses
Suffolk, UK

'*The* place, emphatically *the place*... at Newmarket is the paddock, or the birdcage, or the saddling enclosure, or the parade, or whatever you like to call it,' enthused writer Nat Gould in 1900.[17] Newmarket's long history – patronised by royalty since 1619 – has seen not only many different monikers applied to its parade rings, but also many changes to their physical environment. Newmarket is, of course, remarkable for the number of parade rings it boasts. Consisting of two racecourses – the Rowley Mile and July Course – it accordingly has two parade and pre-parade ring complexes, each very different in character.

Plans for a paddock enclosure at Newmarket were first made in 1858. Since the 1750s, Newmarket had been the home of the Jockey Club and its physical evolution had been much conditioned by providing facilities for its officials and the horsemen, rather than to attract spectators. The paddock too was born of this spirit: 'The Stewards of the Jockey Club propose to... build

a commodious stand,' the *York Herald* reported in 1858,

> with a capacious weighing room, a room for the jockeys, a room for the press, and a room for the Jockey Club on the ground floor, and at the back of the stand a saddling stable, with six stalls. This will be enclosed with a railed yard for the horses to come in to be weighed after all the races which terminate on the flat.[2]

Positioned just after the Rowley Mile finish, it was in use by the early 1860s.[19] It was initially proposed to circumscribe the area with iron railings, but this plan being abandoned as too costly, it was instead enclosed with a wire fence which gave rise to the paddock's unusual nickname, the 'birdcage'.

The birdcage, according to a newspaper account in 1874 was,

> a paddock railed off with wire, to a height of seven feet. Most of the horses are saddled here, and all are brought within it after the race, so the cognoscenti gather around it, or enter if they are of the elite, to criticise the performers in the coming struggle.[20]

As typified paddocks of that era, it was an informal arrangement. For many years, horses were not necessarily saddled there. Horse boxes lined one side, while horses, horsemen and onlookers jostled casually against each other. Jockey Club members, owners and trainers had licence to enter as they pleased, although for others entry was conditional upon a paid ticket. Although long since gone, the birdcage is remembered today in the name of a residential street, Birdcage Walk, close to its erstwhile location.

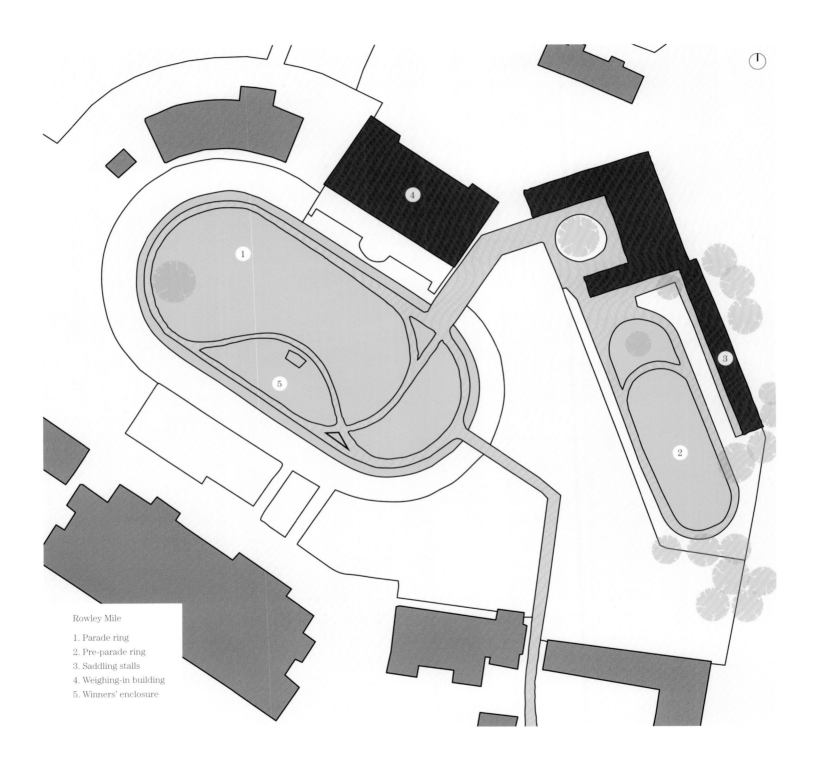

Rowley Mile

1. Parade ring
2. Pre-parade ring
3. Saddling stalls
4. Weighing-in building
5. Winners' enclosure

Above: Rowley Mile, as
photographed in 1933. By 1925,
its paddock contained both a
defined parade ring and pre-
parade ring positioned at the
eastern end of the stands

Opposite: In 1968, the
Rowley Mile rings were
relocated to the rear of
the stands. The current
arrangement dates to
the 1980s

By 1886, the July Course had also been given its own demarcated saddling paddock, in which sat a weighing room. Although both were progressively enlarged, little changed in the layout of either the Rowley Mile or July paddocks until the early 1920s. In this decade, railed oval parade rings were added to the enclosures, in common with other racecourses up and down the country. By 1925, the Rowley Mile paddock also boasted a circular pre-parade ring adjacent to the main ring.[21]

In 1968, a reorganisation took place at the Rowley Mile to render the paddock complex more accessible to racegoers. The two rings were relocated from the eastern end of the stands alongside the track to the rear of them, a far more convenient position for attendees of the Silver Ring enclosure. The orientation of the weighing room was reversed to allow the entrance to face the new ring. Spacious terracing too was erected at the rear of the Silver Ring and main stand overlooking it.[22]

A phased redevelopment beginning in 1987 created the Rowley Mile paddock area that exists today. Stepped terracing was added around the main ring accommodating 8,000, thereby improving spectator sightlines. However, the new layout was not universally welcomed. The weighing room was re-sited on the far side of the ring, lengthening the passage of movement and channels of communication from the stands, while its red brick architecture was lacklustre in spirit.

The July Course paddock, meanwhile, has long been regarded as the most atmospheric scene in Newmarket. This effect does not come from its surrounding buildings – a simple saddling shed and white tented bars – but from its verdant setting. 'If you wish to see a perfectly picturesque birdcage, you can only find it in the glorious plantation on the far side of the July course,' wrote Melbourne newspaper *The Argus* in 1923. '[T]here is nothing so lovely as to sit beneath the leafy boscage of the wood, sheltered from the blazing sun of the dog days, and contentedly watch the mighty thoroughbreds as they walk around the shady paths.'[23]

Notwithstanding a £10-million renovation of the July Course's facilities in 2007, the two rings have changed little since this account was written. The main parade ring sits alongside the track; at the far end, the saddling boxes are roofed with rustic thatch. Behind it, the sylvan pre-parade ring remains a tree-shaded haven. 'The pre-parade ring, shadowy and secretive even on the sunniest of days, is shrouded by trees as tall as in a forest,' wrote Laura Thompson of the July Course in her history of Newmarket, 'among which the horses tread as if in a rustic fairy-tale, their whinnies sliding up through the branches and shivering in the air.'[24] Its intimate tranquillity makes for a vivid contrast with the action on the track.

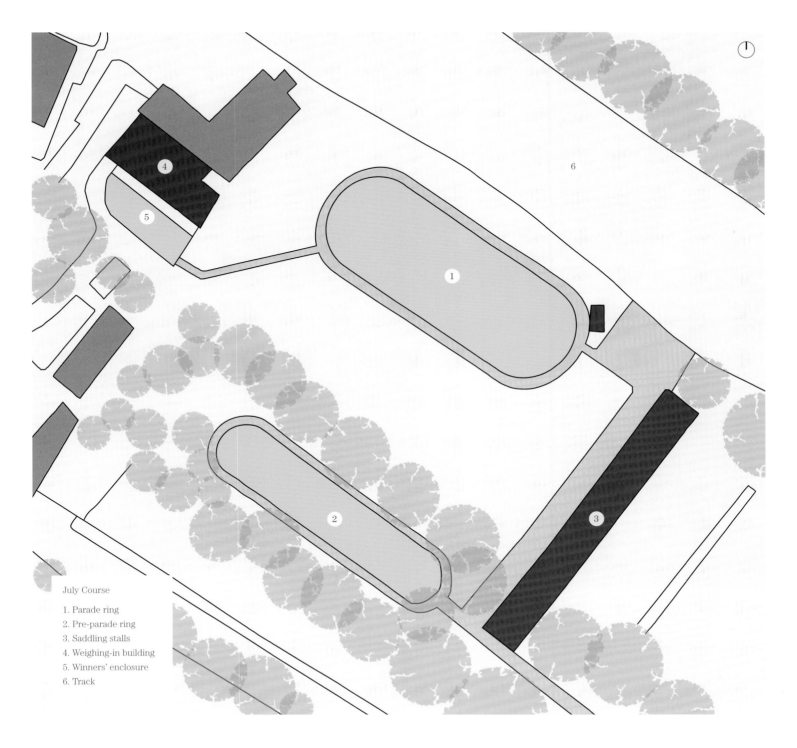

July Course

1. Parade ring
2. Pre-parade ring
3. Saddling stalls
4. Weighing-in building
5. Winners' enclosure
6. Track

Above: The July Course's
pre-parade ring is
routinely hailed for its
sylvan tranquillity

Opposite: The July
Course's parade ring has
changed little since the
1920s when a simple
ringed enclosure was
first installed

Royal Randwick
Sydney, Australia

The 'Theatre of the Horse' is billed as a feature that will expand the racecourse's non-racing remit. The open-air amphitheatre has been planned as a venue capable of hosting concerts, fashion shows and corporate hospitality events. Its primary function, however, is as a focal point for the Randwick race day.

2013 saw the inauguration of a grand new parading complex at Randwick. Christened the 'Theatre of the Horse', it is an outdoor amphitheatre capable of accommodating 4,500 spectators. This format and scale were a first for an Australian racecourse. It was designed as part of a large-scale facelift at Randwick intended to boost its prestige both nationally and internationally.

For the ring's design, Randwick turned to global precedents for inspiration, most notably Ascot. Echoing the arrangement there, Randwick's ring is located to the rear of a new grandstand, constructed simultaneously, from which viewing decks at every level overlook the ring. The ring had previously been located to the front of the 1960s Queen Elizabeth II Grandstand and nineteenth-century Official Stand. It was a wedge-shaped enclosure squeezed in the space between the buildings and the track. The relocation not only created more space for spectators to watch the pre- and post-race parades, but also replicated the nineteenth-century location of Randwick's first saddling paddock.

The new arrangement sees horses process from stalls to the south, and around the ring, before moving through a tunnel under the new grandstand to the track. Patrons can view the spectacle from the tiered standing decks and tiered seating which surround all sides of the ring. Owners and media were not forgotten in the new arrangement either. It includes a purpose-built broadcast studio looking directly onto the turf, and an owners' pavilion on its southern side, consisting of lounges and dining facilities and built using glass, concrete and timber to complement the aesthetic of the grandstand.

The precinct is not without its critics. Many have lamented the loss of an early twentieth-century Tea House that stood on the site of the present ring, while others have raised concerns that the enclosure is too small to host big fields, such as those drawn by the Doncaster Handicap. The new facilities were not officially launched until October 2013, though, and thus are still proving their long-term mettle. It is up to time to tell how successful Randwick's new parade ring will be and whether it will win the support of the track's veteran racegoers.

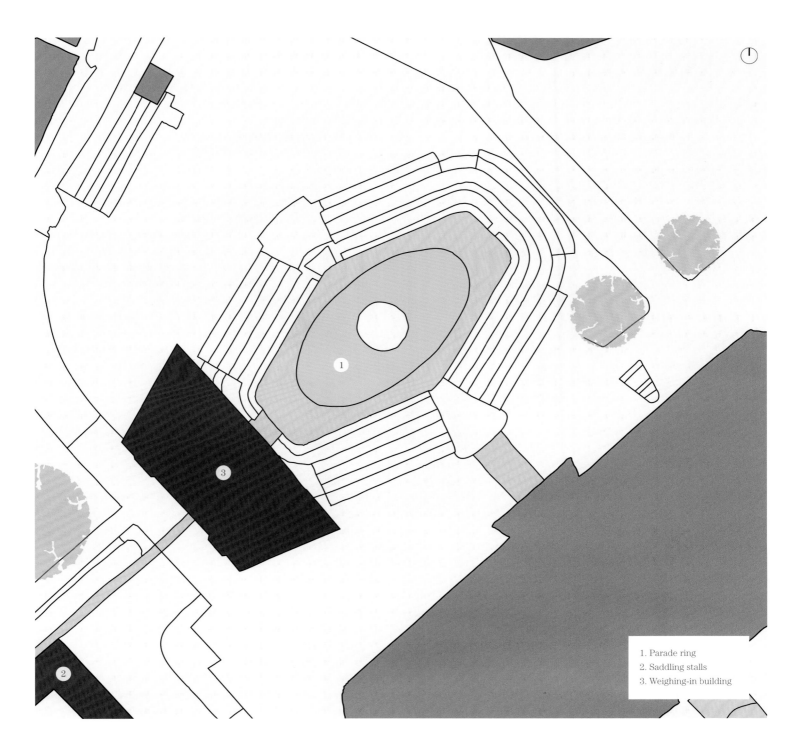

1. Parade ring
2. Saddling stalls
3. Weighing-in building

Above: The parade ring,
or mounting yard, in
front of the nineteenth-
century Official Stand,
photographed in 1937

Opposite: The parade
ring – now named the
Theatre of the Horse –
was relocated (amidst
some controversy) to the
rear of the stands in 2013

Santa Anita Park
California, USA

From its opening day in 1934, Santa Anita Park was designed to be the world's most luxurious racecourse. So intent were its founders upon this goal that, by the time its doors opened for the first time, so much money had been lavished on its construction that none was left for the ticket sellers to make change.

The paddock gardens were conceived as the new track's dazzling entrance experience. The paddock enclosure was designed as a French-inspired, landscaped garden covering two and a half hectares (six acres). Geometrically laid out with parterres, allées of trees, and box hedge-lined walkways, it was unusual for its formality. At its centre was an elliptical walking ring encircled by a wooden cross-bar fence, from which extended radial pathways that aligned with the grandstand's three entrances to the north. At the western end of the gardens stood a semi-circular range of saddling stalls.

Quickly, however, this arrangement began to evolve. By 1938, Santa Anita's popularity necessitated an expansion of the grandstand. The stand was doubled in size with a western addition featuring a central entry pavilion, directly opposite the original saddling barn. The stalls were demolished to create an axial approach to the new entrance, and in their place was placed a fountain set in the centre of a square lawn demarcated at each corner by a single palm tree. A replacement saddling barn, long and narrow with a central classical entrance portico, was erected along the southern edge of the parade ring. A public viewing gallery was installed inside overlooking the horses as they were warmed up and saddled.

The paddock gardens and saddling barn have since been expanded in size, statues have been added, and benches now line the pathways and parterres. Yet, in all other respects, the parade ring that greets visitors upon their entrance today is that which existed in 1938. Horses still process from the stables to the west, via the round receiving barn where horses are inspected and tested, along a tree-lined path to the walking ring and saddling barn. Patrons still press into the barn to glimpse the ritual or gather around the low wooden fence to watch the horses circle the ring. This degree of continuity is unusual, and Santa Anita is celebrated as a place where the spirit of the 1930s can still be experienced.

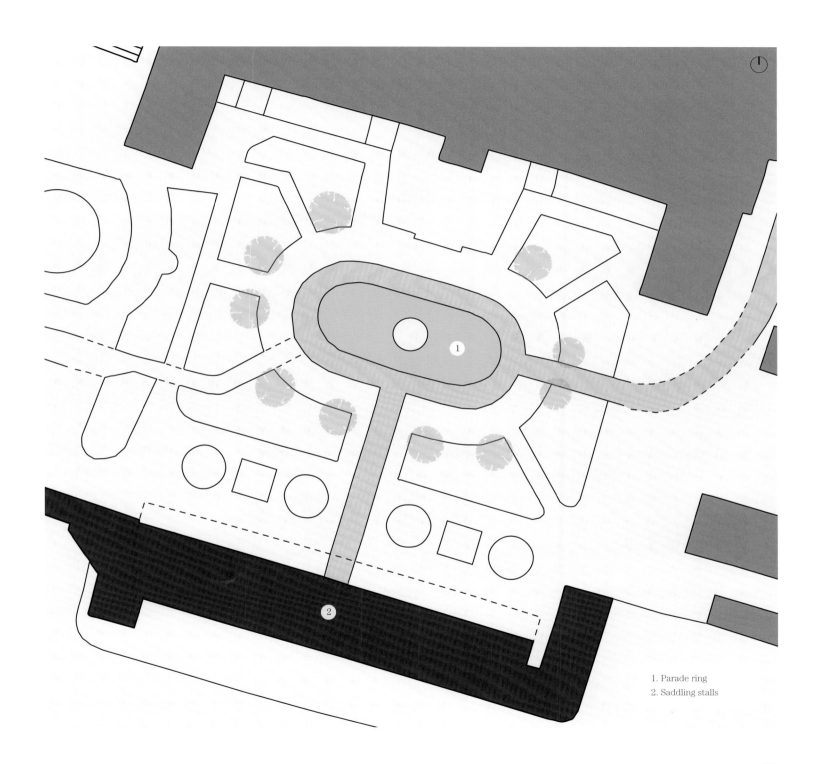

1. Parade ring
2. Saddling stalls

Above: Opened in 1934,
enormous care was
lavished on Santa Anita's
landscape, particularly
that of the paddock

Opposite: The parading
experience at Santa Anita
has changed little since
the 1930s

Saratoga Race Course
New York, USA

'The saddling paddock at Saratoga is the most picturesque in the country,' rhapsodised *The New York Tribune*. 'The horses are scattered about among clumps of trees and between beds of flowers.'[25] Although written in 1902, this account is as true today as ever. The saddling and walking of horses under the verdant canopy of Saratoga's paddock is one of the most cherished scenes within the American racing circuit.

The paddock is one of the oldest surviving features of the historic track, which dates to 1864. Late nineteenth-century maps show the site as a vast lawn peppered with trees, through which horses would meander on their way from the stabling area to the track. It was a simple, bucolic setting. The acreage was gradually reduced in size, and yet for the most part the area remained unchanged until the second half of the twentieth century.

Here, horses would be saddled surrounded by the racetrack community of jockeys, grooms, trainers, owners and clientele. Anyone and everyone could get within touching distance of the equine stars; no fences separated the public. Jockeys passed through the crowds en route to finding their mounts. The groves of vertiginous trees that populated the paddock served as informal stalls and exercise rings. White boards with red numbers were affixed to each tall tree, which acted as the fulcrums of improvised walking circles.

This rustic idyll served as the backdrop for the pre-race preparations, unless of course rain drove it under the cover of the saddling shed. Containing 25 stalls, the large timber shed was built in 1902 as part of a major series of improvements that also saw the track rotated, the grandstand enlarged, and the landscape beautified. Measuring 73 by 22 metres (240 by 72 feet), its dark interior, scent-laden with the smell of straw, was illuminated by a row of louvered small triangular windows set into the roof. It was here that the horses were saddled and paraded on wet-weather days while spectators looked on. 'This commingling of fans, horsepeople and horses was almost unique and one of the loveliest traditions in American sports,' wrote Saratoga historian Edward Hotaling.[26]

The shed once stood at the heart of the paddock, but over time the extent of the paddock was pared away to make room for the growing numbers of picnickers and pleasure makers in the Back Yard – Saratoga's pastoral public garden behind the grandstand – and

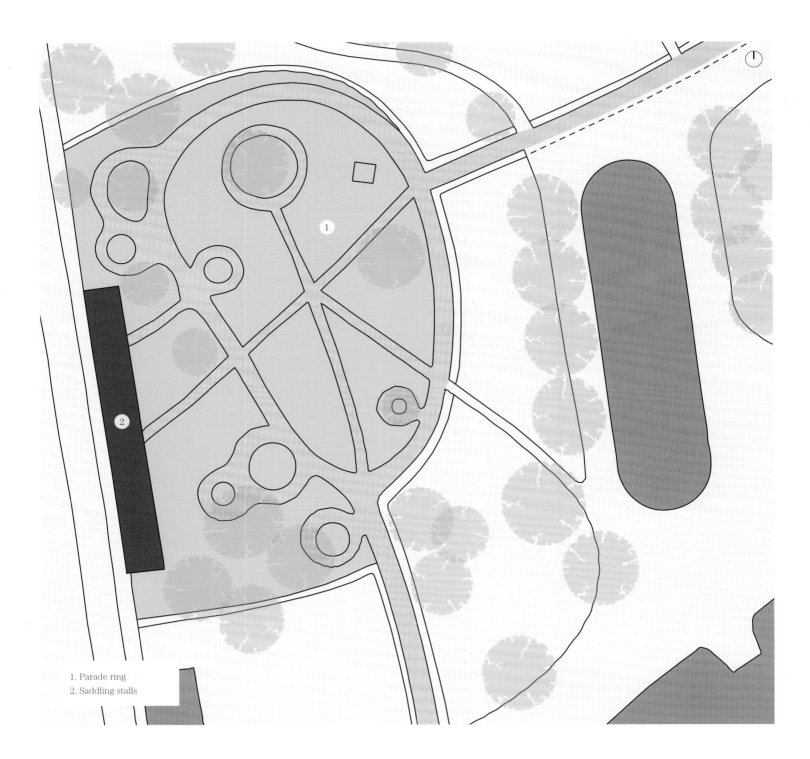

1. Parade ring
2. Saddling stalls

the pre-race rite was edged further
to the west of the site. These changes
were accompanied by more radical
adjustments. In 1963, the 1902 saddling
shed was converted into a pari-mutuel
and office facility. In 1977, a new
saddling tent was erected alongside the
western perimeter of the enclosure.

For so many years, the saddling of
champions under the lofty tree canopy
where turf amateurs could rub elbows
with jockeys and horses had held a
staunch place in Saratoga tradition. It
was now an age of litigation, however,
and it was no longer considered safe
to allow unrestricted public access to
the horses for fear of injury. By 1986
a definite end was put to the custom
when, principally to protect onlookers
from loose horses, the walking ring and
saddling tent were completely enclosed
by white fencing, thereby creating the
paddock that exists now. The forfeiture
was keenly mourned by many.[27]

Although the paddock is no longer open
to the public, the saddling and parading
ritual still takes place under a verdant
canopy of pines. At its centre, stands a
life-size bronze of 1993 Kentucky Derby
and Travers Stakes winner Sea Hero,
which proudly surveys today's runners
and complements the pastoral, festal
atmosphere of yesteryear that still
pervades. The ebullient red-and-white
striped canopy of the saddling tent
and the sylvan backdrop of trees and
flowers makes Saratoga's paddock a
place of celebration.

Right: Saratoga's tree-
shaded parade ring
makes for one of racing's
most atmospheric
destinations

Above: This 1940s photograph
shows the pre-race communion
in the paddock. Tall trees
served as informal stalls and
exercise rings, and no fences
separated the public

Opposite: The preparation of the
thoroughbreds under a canopy of
trees remains a Saratoga tradition,
although now health and safety
fears mean the public are now held
behind white picket fencing

Sha Tin Racecourse
Hong Kong

Horse racing did not become professional in Hong Kong until 1971, but within a few short years its racing, prize-money and local popularity soared, transforming it into one of the world's most important centres for thoroughbred wagering. The city-state's first racecourse, Happy Valley, had opened in 1842 but by the mid 1970s it had outgrown its own success and, in 1978, the Hong Kong Jockey Club opened Sha Tin.

Unlike many of the courses considered here, Sha Tin's parade ring has remained in the same position directly to the rear of the grandstand throughout its, albeit relatively short, lifetime. However, in 2004 it was subject to a grand remodelling. At a cost of HK$400 million and taking 18 months to construct, the project featured new fixed tiered seating, owners' pavilion, balconies extending from the rear of the grandstand, and an artificial turf surface. The focus of the scheme, however, was the installation of a retractable roof – the world's first at a racecourse.

The roof allows horses, horsemen and racing fans to experience the parade in comfort, providing shade from the sun and protection during the rainy season. Spanning 126 metres in length and reaching a height of 42 metres (413 by 138 feet), it covers an area of 13,000 square metres (140,000 square feet). The working principle is to create a cover over the ring by the sliding of two roof panels in opposite directions. The closing/opening of the panels takes approximately seven to eight minutes to accomplish. In wet weather the roof provides shelter from the rain, and if it is too hot the temperature is controlled using spot cooling.

The racecourse as a whole can accommodate huge audiences of up to 85,000 spectators, and special attention has been shown by the Jockey Club to ensure as many as possible of these can experience the parade ring at first hand. Patrons can view the ring from 1,400 fixed tiered seats and four balconies. The 2004 redevelopment increased the spectator capacity of the area from 2,324 to 4,700.

The aim of the project was to make the pre-race experience at Sha Tin a superlative one. 'At a time when our turnover was falling,' explained Hong Kong Jockey Club's executive director of racing, Winfried Engelbrecht-Bresges, in 2004, 'we felt we needed to take the racecourse to a whole new dimension and invest in our facilities for the future'.[28]

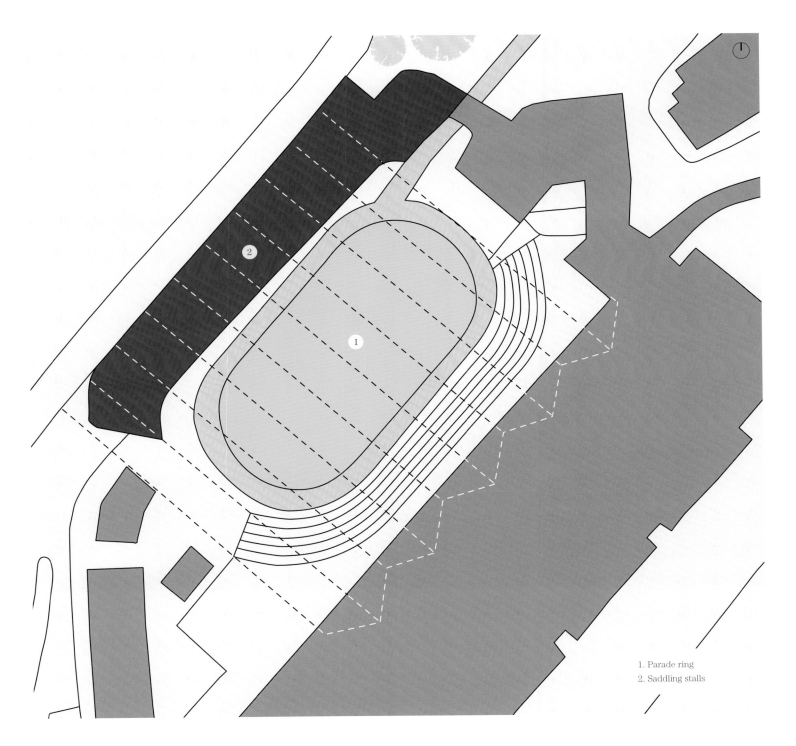

1. Parade ring
2. Saddling stalls

Above: Hong Kong's
second racecourse was
opened in 1978 with a
parade ring sited directly
behind its grandstand

Opposite: In 2004, Sha Tin
installed a world's first – a
retractable roof over the
parade ring, added to ensure
comfort in all weathers

Singapore Racecourse
Kranji, Singapore

The city-state of Singapore has a long racing heritage. Its first turf club was founded in 1842, and the following year a racecourse opened. The island's current track is of much more recent genesis though. Opened in 1999, the complex was built anew on an empty site. Examples of the wholesale construction of racecourses in recent decades are few and far between, and it is insightful that when they were presented with this opportunity the Singapore Turf Club opted to position the parade ring at the heart of the racegoers' experience.

The ring was designed to be a hub of movement, energy and colour. At the Turf Club's previous home, the enclosure had been situated in front of the grandstand. However, to enhance accessibility and anticipating layouts later implemented during redevelopments at Ascot and Chantilly, at the new racecourse the parade ring was placed directly behind the grandstand. The Turf Club saw it as a priority that spectators should be able to engage with the pre-race activities, and that the setting should, through its design, cultivate an aura of pageantry and expectation.

The realised product is an oval ring where the horses are saddled, exercised, and mounted. It is framed on one side by 26 covered, timber-lined saddling stalls, and by tiered concrete steps on the other. The original design saw the steps sheltered by what was the most distinctive feature of the enclosure – 60 white sun canopies held aloft by a bright yellow frame. The Teflon-coated white panels fanned out in different directions like the wings of birds, creating a joyous motif which complemented the festive nature of the parade ring. In fulfilling their raison d'être to protect those watching the ring from equatorial showers and the powerful sun, however, they did not prove altogether successful. With the designers underestimating the extent of the locality's downpours, spectators often found themselves getting wet and the horses were not shielded at all. As a result, in 2012 the canopies were replaced with a sweeping, steel-framed Teflon roof that was erected over the entire enclosure. The result is an all-weather environment for both the participants and viewers of the ring.

The tiered platforms offer obstruction-free viewing for large numbers of spectators to watch the horses circulate the oval. The procession then continues through a highly successful design feature: a glass-sided horse-walk running from the ring, through the grandstand and to the track. A glazed weighing room and official's room flank each side of the walk. Each stage of the pre-race ritual is thus celebrated at Singapore in an environment that has been consciously designed to facilitate, enhance and celebrate the aesthetic experience of the race day.

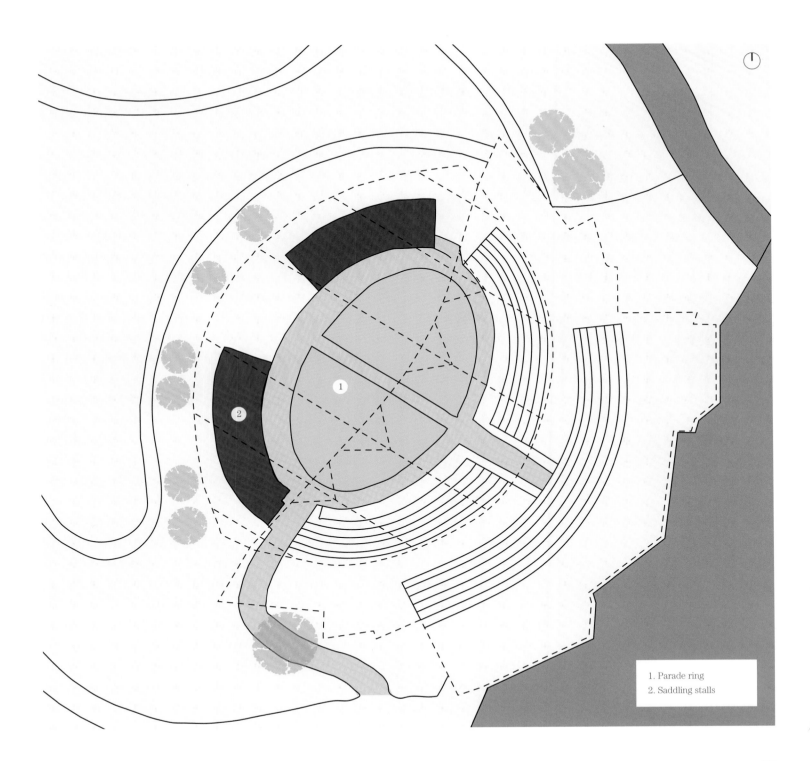

1. Parade ring
2. Saddling stalls

Above: Built in 1999, the state-of-the-art Singapore Racecourse placed its oval parade ring at the heart of the race-day experience

Opposite: In 2012, the parade ring was renovated with new Teflon canopies for the comfort of horses, horsemen and spectators in Singapore's tropical weather

York Racecourse
Yorkshire, UK

York Racecourse has a prestigious place in the chronology of racecourse design, for it was here, in 1756, that the first modern grandstand of any sport was opened. Since then each generation has left its mark on the built environment, including its parade ring.

York's saddling paddock was created in 1875, part of the mid-nineteenth-century trend amongst British racecourses to formalise and order the race-day procedures by setting aside a designated area for the horses' toilette. It was sited in much the same position in which the parade ring stands today, at the north end of the stands alongside the track. It was an open, unfenced lawn where horses, horsemen and racegoers intermingled unceremoniously. The enclosure came complete with a two-storey structure (that still stands today) housing a weighing room below and viewing accommodation above for owners and trainers. In the ensuing years the paddock grew in size to the north and east, and was augmented by new buildings, both temporary and permanent. It was enlarged as early as 1876, and again in 1895 when saddling boxes were erected at the northern perimeter. Some three years later, the area was enclosed.

A major expansion came in the early twentieth century when, in 1907, the York Race Committee acquired additional land to the east of its original holdings. The bounding road was realigned and a new perimeter wall was built in 1908, approximately doubling the paddock's size. An impressive gateway complete with rusticated dressed-stone piers capped with classical urns was inserted at its northern end; in the southern section, a stand-alone weighing room was built against the new wall; while alongside it, the ground-floor arcade of the original 1756 grandstand was relocated from its trackside position and re-erected against the boundary wall to serve as a bar.

By the early 1920s, a railed parade ring had been added in the paddock next to the track. In 1971, after several enlargements, the ring was given an unusual addition – elevated seating held aloft upon concrete pillars was built around it. The structure accommodated 1,000 people and was part of an extensive raised walkway that stretched along the rear length of York's stands.

This elevated seating was removed in 1998, but in other respects York's parade ring area and its ancillary structures of saddling boxes, arcade bar and weighing room were left unchanged. That is until 2013, when work began on a phased redevelopment project to transform the northern end of the racecourse.

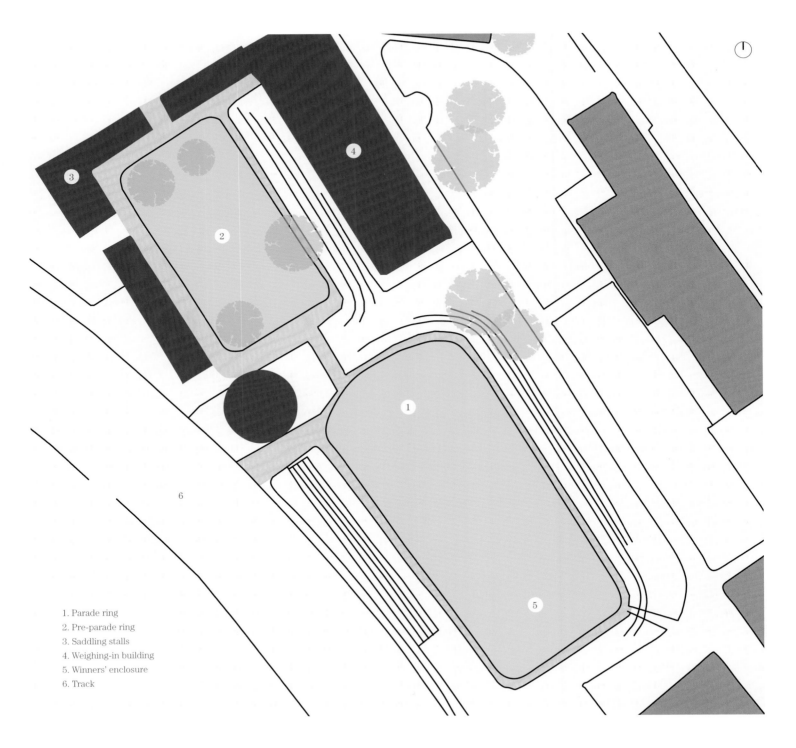

1. Parade ring
2. Pre-parade ring
3. Saddling stalls
4. Weighing-in building
5. Winners' enclosure
6. Track

Opposite: By the mid-twentieth century, York's paddock had two clearly demarcated rings for the pre-parade and parade

Over the years, as the racecourse and its attendances grew, the paddock area had become less efficient. Firstly, to go to and from the pre-parade ring, northeast of the main ring, horses were led through a busy part of the racecourse intersecting a spectator footpath; stewards had to block this route to racegoers throughout the day to allow horse traffic to cross. Secondly, the Edwardian weighing room had become cramped by modern standards and was remote from the parade ring, meaning jockeys were forced to jostle their way through spectator crowds before mounting. Moreover, the stalls and pre-parade area were simply too small to be functional. York's stables are located on the opposite side of the track, and as a consequence horses have to travel from here to the pre-parade ring approximately an hour before their race. Frequently, entrants from two different races are held in the pre-parade precinct at the same time, and on several occasions accidents had been narrowly avoided. The redevelopment enabled York to address these issues by consolidating the equine facilities.

In 2014, the pre-parade ring was relocated westwards. Its previous site was converted into expanded hospitality facilities for patrons, and a larger replacement was built immediately to the north of the main parade ring alongside the track. Surrounded by modern timber saddling boxes, veterinary rooms and wash-down areas, the new rectangular pre-parade precinct has been warmly welcomed by trainers and stable staff. The arrangement has reduced the congestion of horses before and after the races, has expedited the horse route from the stables to pre-parade ring and has obviated crossing points between horses and racegoers. The enclosed courtyard space created by the boxes screens the ring from the action on the adjacent track, thereby conducing the quiet atmosphere desirable for the pre-parade activities.

The latter is also aided by the positioning of the new weighing-in building. Sited on the eastern perimeter of the pre-parade ring, the structure is both easily accessible from the two rings and serves as a physical buffer between the noise of the spectator areas and the pre-parade ring. Containing commodious jockeys' and officials' accommodation on the ground floor and a restaurant above, its updated facilities have been welcomed by horsemen and racegoers alike. Not all is modern though – the building makes a nostalgic nod to the racecourse's architectural heritage by echoing the cast-iron barber poles and fretwork of the nineteenth-century grandstand.

Although the main parade ring itself has remained untouched, the scheme brings the greatest change to the paddock area for over a century, and has enhanced York's appeal both for its horsemen and for its patrons.

Above: The paddock in 1909 was an open, unfenced area where patrons, horses and horsemen intermixed freely

Opposite: In 2014, a comprehensive remodelling relocated the pre-parade ring directly north of the main ring, improving safety, equine facilities and spectator viewing

Notes

FASHIONS, FORMS AND FUNCTIONS

1 The authors are indebted to Tim Cox and John Pinfold for this information. The parade ring at Gatwick was certainly in place by 1903. As with many of the other tracks discussed here, it is difficult to be totally precise with dates. The little-studied nature of parade rings means that source material is scant, and the authors have relied heavily on references within newspaper reports to establish chronological data throughout the book.

2 *Baily's Magazine of Sports & Pastimes*, vol. 87, May 1907, 419.

3 *The North Wales Chronicle*, 7 August 1833.

4 *The Bury and Norwich Post*, 25 May 1831.

5 *Wiltshire Independent*, 3 August 1837.

6 *Morning Chronicle*, 13 June 1838; *Worcester Journal*, 2 August 1838.

7 J. Kent, *Racing Life of Lord George Cavendish Bentinck and Other Reminiscences*, Edinburgh: W. Blackwood, 1892, pp. 296-7; M. Huggins, *Flat Racing and British Society 1790-1914*, London: Frank Cass, 2000, p. 123.

8 It should be noted that although Australian and New Zealand tracks tend to follow the British practice of having two separate rings, the pre-race routines are not identical to those of the UK. In New Zealand, current practice is to saddle horses in tie-ups or day stables before they enter the first ring.

9 R. Sheard, *Sports Architecture*, London: Spon Press, 2001, p. 13.

10 Personal correspondence with authors, 12 January 2015.

CASE STUDIES

1 World Buildings Directory: Aintree Racecourse. Online. http://www.worldbuildingsdirectory.com/project.cfm?id=603 (accessed 3/12/14).

2 M. Spring, 'A Different Beast', *Building*, no. 12, March 2007, 40-4; 'BDP's redevelopment of Aintree', *Architecture Today*, no. 178, May 2007, 83-4.

3 *Morning Chronicle*, 13 June 1838.

4 D. Laird, *Royal Ascot*, London: Hodder and Stoughton, 1976, pp. 121-2.

5 W.S. Vosburgh, *Racing in America 1866-1921*, New York: The Jockey Club, 1922, p. 34.

6 P. Roberts and I. Taylor, *Racecourse Architecture*, New York: Acanthus Press, 2013, pp. 218-21.

7 N. Stout, *Great American Thoroughbred Racetracks*, New York: Rizzoli, 1991, p. 63.

8 *Maryborough Chronicle, Wide Bay and Burnett Advertiser*, 17 October 1887.

9 C. Cecil, G. Ennor, and R. Onslow, *Glorious Goodwood*, Westbourne: Kenneth Mason Publications, 2002, p. 182.

10 C. Donati, *Michael Hopkins*, Milan: Skira, 2006, p. 152; M. Summerfield, 'Glorious Goodwood', *The Architectural Review*, vol. 211, February 2002, 56-9.

11 A. W. Kinglake, *The Invasion of the Crimea*, vol. 1, Edinburgh and London: William Blackwood & Sons, 1901, p. 222.

12 R. Romanet-Riondet and G. Thibault, *Centenaire de la Société d'Encouragement 1833-1933 et Les Heures Mouvementées de la Société d'Encouragement 1993-1991*, Boulogne: Castelet, 1993, p. 179.

13 'A Proposal for the Establishment of a Model Race Track at Keeneland', unpublished report, nd. [1935], p. 5.

14 *Keeneland: A Thoroughbred Legacy*, Lexington: Blood-Horse Publications/Keeneland Association, 2010, p. 48.

15 Ibid., pp. 25-6.

16 V. Mitchell, 'Keeneland: Building on a Solid Foundation', *BloodHorse*, 1 October 2011, 2646.

17 N. Gould, *Sporting Sketches*, London: R. A. Everett & Co., 1900, p. 30.

18 *York Herald*, 24 December 1858.

19 The authors are indebted to Tim Cox for this information.

20 *The Sheffield Daily Telegraph*, 19 October 1874.

21 The circular pre-parade ring had been altered to an oval shape by the late 1920s.

22 R. Onslow, *Headquarters: A History of Newmarket and its Racing*, Cambridge: Great Ouse Press, 1983, pp. 274-5.

23 *The Argus*, 7 November 1923.

24 L. Thompson, *Newmarket: From James I to the Present Day*, London: Virgin Publishing Ltd, 2000, p. 8.

25 *The New York Tribune*, 5 August 1902.

26 E. Hotaling, *They're Off! Horse Racing at Saratoga*, Syracuse: Syracuse University Press, 1995, p. 275.

27 P. Roberts and I. Taylor, *The Spa: Saratoga's Legendary Race Course*, London: Turnberry Consulting, 2011, pp. 106-7.

28 *South China Morning Post*, 4 November 2004.

Picture Credits

10 Library of Congress, Prints & Photographs Division, FSA/OWI Collection [LC-USF34-057458-E]; 14, 17 Timothy Cox; 16 Trustees of the British Museum; 18, 70, 74 State Library of Victoria; 20, 101 Thoroughbred Photography Ltd; 22 Amie Karlsson; 24 Library of Congress, Prints & Photographs Division, FSA/OWI Collection [LC-DIG-npcc-09652]; 25 Southern California Edison Archive, courtesy of the Huntington Library, San Marino, CA; 27, 136 Dennis Gilbert; 32, 79 Sealand Aerial Photography Ltd; 34 Jane Clarke; 35 David Barbour/ BDP; 38, 50, 104, 121 Turnberry Consulting; 39 Chuck Eckert; 43, 100 Historic England; 44 John Bailey; 45 Miles Willis/Getty Images for Ascot Racecourse; 46 Steve Bardens/Getty Images; 51 Susie Raisher; 52, 118 Adam Coglianese; 56 Herald Post Collection, 1994.18, Photographic Archives, University of Louisville, Louisville, Kentucky; 57 AP Photo/Darron Cummings; 60 Club Hipico de Santiago; 61 Luis Molina; 64 Del Mar Turf Club; 65-6, 113 Horsephotos.com; 71 Steriline Racing; 75 Richard I'Anson; 78 West Sussex Records Office; 80 Mike Caldwell; 84 Jean Stern; 85 aprh.fr; 88 The Art Archive/Chateau Lafitte France/Gianni Dagli Orti; 89 Copyleft; 93 Keeneland Library; 94 University of Kentucky; 95-6 Keeneland Association; 105 www.markwestleyphotography.com; 108 State Library of New South Wales; 109 AAP Image/ Dean Lewins; 112 Los Angeles Public Library; 116, 120 Bolster Collection, Saratoga Springs History Museum; 124 Thierry Orban/Sygma/Corbis; 125 Michael Elleray; 128 Mark Dadswell/Getty Images; 129 See Chee Keong Photography; 133-5 York Racecourse.

Front cover: *York Racecourse*, Dennis Gilbert; Back cover: *Flemington Racecourse*, State Library of Victoria; page 2: *Doncaster Racecourse*, Timothy Cox; page 4: *York Racecourse*, York Racecourse; page 12: *Goodwood Racecourse*, Timothy Cox; page 28: *Keeneland Race Course*, Keeneland Association; page 140: *Hippodrome de Chantilly*, aprh.fr; page 142: *Goodwood Racecourse*, Alan Crowhurst/ Getty Images.

Acknowledgements

The authors are indebted to the help of many people in the preparation of this book. Many individuals and racecourses have offered invaluable assistance in compiling the information and photographs that have gone into its making, and to all those we extend our thanks.

Thanks go to Brendan Phelan, Timothy Cox, Luis Molina, James Parillo, John Pinfold, Paul Henderson, Jane Clarke, Rod Pindar, York Racecourse, Del Mar Thoroughbred Club, Keeneland Association, Keeneland Library and many others.

Special acknowledgements go to Dave Gibson of Draught Associates for designing the book and Benni Allen for preparing the plans that feature within each of the case studies.

Index